Seeing the Smithsonian

THE OFFICIAL GUIDEBOOK TO THE SMITHSONIAN INSTITUTION
ITS MUSEUMS AND GALLERIES

The Smithsonian Institution
A Special Publication

Designed, produced and distributed by the
CBS/EDUCATION & PUBLISHING GROUP

Library of Congress Catalog Number: 73-3003

Printed in the United States of America

ISBN 03-011316-4

Contents

Welcome to the Smithsonian Institution

Many of you come to the Nation's Capital with a sense of excitement and awe, for here is the center of our government with all its attendant glamour and complexity. You have heard of the Smithsonian and believe that it, too, is something you should see during your visit. We share that belief—we think it is a "must" for the visitor to Washington. And we want to help you enjoy it in every way possible.

So, this Guide is designed for you, whether you are from Maine or Oklahoma, Hawaii or Idaho. You come from all fifty states, and from all over the world, as well. Usually your first questions are, "What is the Smithsonian?"; "Is it just one red brick building?"; "How can I see the things I want to?"

Within these pages we have tried to summarize the scope and activities of this great complex of museums and scholarly research. Established as an Institution for "the increase and diffusion of knowledge among men," the Smithsonian carries on this concept through its collections, its conservation efforts, and its publications. As a visitor you will be concerned only with the things you may see, touch, listen to, climb upon, or walk into. But we hope you will be aware of the marvelous behind-the-scenes elements of the Smithsonian that use the talents of many hundreds of people to bring to the foreground the objects which some 15 million of you come to look at annually.

If it is truly active and reflective of its own time, a museum will, like any living thing, change and grow. Although we are constantly changing, we have selected the outstanding and permanent items to feature in this Guide. We hope you will discover the things you want to see, that you will enjoy looking and learning with us, and that you may consider further participation in our activities through membership in the Smithsonian Associates described inside the back cover of this book.

Welcome, then, and have a good time!

S. Dillon Ripley

S. Dillon Ripley
Secretary

The Smithsonian... What Is It?

S. DILLON RIPLEY, Secretary

Original Building

The Mall: South side at 10th St., S.W.

Open: Daily except Christmas
(Great Hall)

Hours: 10:00 a.m. to 5:30 p.m.

Telephone: (202) 628-4422.)

What you should know about the Smithsonian

Admission is free to all museums, galleries, and the Zoo.

How to find your way around
Each museum and gallery has its own *information desks,* manned from 10:00 a.m. to 4:00 p.m. by volunteers who will be glad to assist with building floor plans, Smithsonian literature, and useful tips in planning the best way to see the things that interest you. And don't hesitate to ask any of our guards for help—they're stationed throughout the buildings.

The Smithsonian Associates Reception Center and Information Desk
Located in the Great Hall, Smithsonian Institution Building

Even if you're not a member of the Associates (see inside back cover), you are cordially invited to use the *information facilities* offered to visitors in the "Castle." Here you will find up-to-date material on all aspects of Smithsonian activities. Brochures describing the Institution are available in English, French, and Spanish.

Members of the Smithsonian Associates are welcome to inquire at the Reception Center about subjects of particular interest to them. Additional information is available on other sites of interest in Washington, including maps; and on shopping, eating, and motels and hotels.

What's available in the museums and galleries
In each section of this guidebook we have included a list of services and facilities offered by that particular museum.

Smithsonian Associates Reception Center in the Great Hall.

Beyond that, you may want to know about:

Where to eat
Pleasant cafeterias are located in The National Museum of History and Technology and the National Gallery of Art. The Smithsonian Commons Dining Room in the Smithsonian Building is open weekdays to members of the staff and the Associates for lunch. Nearby is "F" Street, the center of downtown Washington. Walk north toward it along any numbered street and you will find a variety of eating places. To the south, across from the Arts and Industries Building, lies the expansive L'Enfant Plaza complex of offices, restaurants, and shops. Seafood restaurants along the Washington waterfront (about a half-mile south of the Mall) are favorites with tourists.

Parking
It's a problem on the Mall. Garage parking is available in L'Enfant Plaza, entering from 10th Street and Independence Avenue, S.W., directly behind the main Smithsonian Building. A pay parking lot is located on 14th Street, between Constitution Avenue and Pennsylvania Avenue.

Museum Shops
Books, postcards and slides, arts and crafts from the four corners of the world, reproductions of paintings, games and puzzles and models are for sale in the ten shops within the major museums and at the Zoo. Look in the museum section of the guidebook for locations within each building.

Public transportation
The Smithsonian is served by public buses along the following routes: 14th Street, Constitution Avenue, Independence Avenue, 7th Street. For route numbers and for additional information, call Metro. Phone: 637-2437.

How to get around
Tourmobile. Specially designed for the visitor, Tourmobiles circle the Mall and Monument areas throughout the day at a nominal charge. Free reboarding during the same day is permitted from eleven stopping points. Information at Tourmobile stops and at the information desks in the museums.

Pets are not permitted in the buildings, or at the Zoo.

For general information about the Smithsonian Institution, write to Office of Public Affairs, Smithsonian Institution, Washington, D.C. 20560, or call one of the following numbers (area code 202):

Central Information Desk 381-6264
Associates Reception Center 381-6264
Central Box Office Ticket information on presentations at the Smithsonian 381-5395
Dial-A-Museum Daily announcements of new exhibits and special events 737-8811
Dial-A-Phenomenon Weekly announcements on stars, planets and worldwide occurrences of short-lived natural phenomena 737-8855

The Mall

In less than one year—between 1791 and 1792—Major Pierre L'Enfant, a French engineer employed by George Washington to formulate a plan for the new Capital City, designed the concept that is largely in evidence today. Bureaucratic problems beset L'Enfant's original plan and it was not until early in this century that it was reestablished, modified, and enlarged.

One of its features was the area known as the Mall—a grassy sweep from the Capitol to the Washington Monument. During the 19th century, though, it would have been difficult to envision the space as it now exists. The Pennsylvania Railroad Station and rundown shacks (some used as Civil War barracks) occupied the land, surrounded by assorted gardens and the pile of stone that was the incomplete Washington Monument. Beyond lay the largest marsh in the city.

In 1902, under the recommendations and guidance of a senatorial commission, work was begun to implement some of the original concept. What you see now is closer to L'Enfant's design than ever before.

Great Hall, Smithsonian Institution Building.

THE SMITHSONIAN Today

The Smithsonian Institution is an independent establishment dedicated to the increase and diffusion of knowledge. It is a great complex of museums and art galleries, scholars, experts—and a good deal more as well. It is devoted to public education, basic research, and national service in the arts, sciences, and history, with major facilities in Washington, around the country, and overseas.

In addition to the museums described in this book, there are a number of other major components of the Smithsonian in Washington. The Radiation Biology Laboratory plays a unique role in the study of the effects of solar radiation. There is the Oceanographic Sorting Center at the

Washington Navy Yard. And a center for advanced study, the Woodrow Wilson International Center for Scholars, has recently been established with offices in the original Smithsonian building. Under a deed from Mrs. Marjorie Merriweather Post, the lovely northwest Washington estate known as Hillwood, with its great Russian and French collections, will in the future become an eighth public art museum.

Smithsonian facilities and activities stretch across the nation and the world. Chief among these installations elsewhere is the Smithsonian Astrophysical Observatory in Cambridge, Massachusetts. The Observatory itself operates installations in other parts of the United States and field stations in several nations around the globe.

Other elements include a conference center in nearby Maryland; a biological research center on the Chesapeake Bay; offices in New York, Detroit, Boston, and San Francisco supporting the work of the Washington-based Archives of American Art; an oceanographic sorting center in Salammbo, Tunisia, whose work parallels the programs of the Institution's oceanographic center in the Washington Navy Yard; one of the world's leading tropical research institutes, centered in Panama; and the Fort Pierce (Florida) Bureau which conducts marine studies and research in a broad range of subjects.

A wide range of programs is conducted in cooperation with other institutions, universities, and government agencies here in the United States and on every continent. The Institution offers its massive facilities and vast intellectual resources for research and education—from the elementary to post-graduate levels in areas of Smithsonian scientific and cultural interest.

More than two thousand scientific expeditions to the far corners of the world have been sponsored or participated in by staff members over the decades. The Smithsonian joins in continuing research projects in many nations abroad, in some cases using United States government surplus commodity funds for this purpose.

For more than a century, the Smithsonian has circulated research and other publications here and abroad in voluminous quantities. Today, a number of its components are engaged in varying aspects of

Library of the Woodrow Wilson Center.

Smithsonian Associates kite-flying contest on the grounds of the Washington Monument.

publication, distribution, exchange, and information-retrieval services. Communications activities also include radio, television, and motion picture programs.

At the same time, the Smithsonian's performing arts activities cover a wide spectrum—puppet shows to classical concerts to a college drama festival. During the Fourth of July holidays, a Festival of American Folklife is presented on the Mall with selective representations annually from various regions of the country.

All told, the Smithsonian has more than three thousand one hundred employees, including a staff of more than three hundred professional scholars and scientists, many of them leading experts in their fields. A dues-paying membership program set up in 1965, the Smithsonian Associates has more than 600,000 members throughout the nation as well as in the Washington area.

The Smithsonian is a national institution, which receives substantial support from the federal government as well as essential funding from private sources, including the endowment of James Smithson that marked the beginning of the Institution.

Business organizations and persons interested in supporting Smithsonian efforts in research, scholarships, and education as described throughout the book are invited to contact the Office of Development for information on Corporate and Contributing Membership in the Associates.

THE SMITHSONIAN— How It Grew

The Smithsonian owes its origin to James Smithson, a wealthy English scientist who never visited this country. Smithson, who died in Italy in 1829, willed his entire fortune to the United States "to found at Washington, under the name of the Smithsonian Institution, an Establishment for the increase and diffusion of knowledge among men." The bequest totaled more than half a million dollars, a great fortune in that day.

Receipt of the bequest in America in 1838 precipitated a lengthy debate in Congress on whether the nation should or indeed legally could accept the funds and the accompanying trust.

Consequently, it created by enactment a discrete corporate entity, "The Establishment," to undertake the charge of the Smithson will. This body, in effect constituting the Smithsonian Institution, consists of the President of the United States, the Vice President, the Chief Justice, and heads of the executive departments.

To govern the Institution thus established, the Board of Regents was created. Reflecting the origins and the dual public and private nature of the Institution, it was to be composed of the Vice President and Chief Justice, three members of the Senate, three members of the House of Representatives, and six citizen members. The Vice President and Chief Justice were named both to the Establishment and the Board of Regents. Of the citizen members, it was stipulated that two must be residents of the District of Columbia and no two of the remaining four may be from the same state. The number of citizen members is now nine.

The position of Secretary of the Smithsonian Institution also was established at the outset, the incumbent serving as well as Secretary of the Board of Regents.

The Smithson bequest was deposited in the United States Treasury. The federal government agreed to pay six percent interest on it to the Smithsonian in perpetuity.

Provision was made in formal creation of the Smithsonian for work in the areas of concern that have since occupied the Institution through succeeding generations—art, science, history, research, museum and library operation, and the dissemination of information.

Congress, in taking action on the Smithson bequest, stated its purpose was to provide "for the faithful execution of said trust agreeable to the will of the liberal and enlightened donor." The United States thus solemnly bound itself to the administration of a trust, and the relations of the federal government to the Smithsonian Institution became that of a guardian to a ward.

The Secretaries

In its long history eight distinguished scholars have served as Secretary. Each has contributed indelibly to the formation and character of the Institution whose own growth and response to scholarly and popular requirements may be looked upon as a microcosm of the growth of the United States for more than a century and a quarter.

Between 1846 and 1878 *Joseph Henry* served as the Institution's first Secretary and it was under his guidance that the Smithsonian's course was set for the widespread increase and dissemination of knowledge dictated by the Smithsonian mandate. Henry was a famed physical scientist, a Princeton University professor, with a mind of remarkable genius. It has been said of him that his discoveries in electromagnetism took up where Ben Franklin left off. Henry fostered the extensive publication program of scientific findings that remains of paramount importance today, and established the basic organization that enabled the Smithsonian to develop its own direction during the mid-19th century.

Spencer Fullerton Baird, a distinguished naturalist, joined the Smithsonian as Assistant Secretary in 1850. He succeeded Joseph Henry as Secretary in 1878, serving until his own death in 1887. Thus, for more than thirty years he exerted significant influence on the Institution's growth. Taking advantage of the many exploratory expeditions then taking place, Baird called upon participants to contribute to the Smithsonian's collections and was thus instrumental in the development of the museums of the Institution.

The third secretary was *Samuel Pierpont Langley*, whose own scientific interests corresponded with the revolutionary developments being made during the time of his service, 1887-1906, in the field of aeronautics, astrophysics, and astronomy. As early as 1896 he built steam-driven aircraft models with thirteen-foot wingspreads that made successful unmanned test flights of one-half to three-quarters of a mile. In 1890 he established the Astrophysical Observatory. His interests also extended to the preservation of animal life, resulting in the founding of the National Zoological Park in 1889, as well as the growth of a collection of art works officially organized in 1906, now known as the National Collection of Fine Arts.

Charles Doolittle Walcott, geologist and paleontologist, had a widespread influence on national scientific matters during the first quarter of this century. Serving as Secretary between 1907 and 1927, he brought into being the National Advisory Committee on Aeronautics; played an important part in the development of forestry and reclamation projects; served as president of the National Academy of Sciences and the American Association for the Advancement of Science. During his administration the Freer Gallery of Art was added to the Smithsonian.

In 1895 a young man named *Charles Greeley Abbot* began serving as an aide to Secretary Langley in the Astrophysical Observatory. His principal researches were on solar radiation and solar power. Becoming Secretary in 1928, he established the Observatory's Division of Radiation and Organisms the following year. During his tenure, which lasted until his retirement in 1944, the National Gallery of Art was added to the Smithsonian as a separate bureau. Remaining active in solar investigations, Dr. Abbot was granted patents in 1968 and in 1972 for apparatuses for converting solar energy to electricity. In May 1972 he was honored by the Board of Regents on the occasion of his 100th birthday.

After twenty years' service as Assistant Secretary, *Dr. Alexander Wetmore* succeeded Dr. Abbot as Secretary in 1945. His studies in ornithology are well known. To the broader aspects of his science he contributed a Systematic Classification for the Birds of the World, monographs on the fossil birds of North America, and monographs and smaller papers on birds of various regions, particularly of Latin America. During his administration of the Smithsonian, two bureaus were added to the organization—the National Air Museum and the Canal Zone Biological Area, now known as the Smithsonian Tropical Research Institution.

A physiological psychologist and former president of Tufts University, *Dr. Leonard Carmichael* was Secretary of the Smithsonian between 1953 and 1964. Rapid growth changed the Institution's public image from "the Nation's attic" to the "Nation's showcase" with the opening of The National Museum of History and Technology. The number of catalogued objects increased to almost 60,000,000 and the annual number of visitors to the Mall reached 10,000,000. In 1958 two significant additions were authorized by Congress: the National Cultural Center was approved (now the separately administered John F. Kennedy Center for the Performing Arts); and the Patent Office Building was transferred to the Smithsonian for eventual use as a home for the National Collection of Fine Arts and the National Portrait Gallery.

Since 1964, under the innovative leadership of incumbent Secretary *S. Dillon Ripley,* biologist, ecologist, and authority on the birds of the Far East, the Institution's responsibilities and participation have extended across a broad spectrum—including education, research, public service, community activities, conservation, and the performing as well as visual arts. Bureaus and other major divisions have been added or revivified. An additional number of distinguished scholars have joined the staff. International symposia and other significant events of international scope have been held.

Rigorous emphasis has been placed on scholarship and research within Secretary Ripley's concept of the Smithsonian as a kind of open university in the manner of the earliest museums of classical times, an approach that also accords with the Institution's traditions from its earliest days. At the same time, his determination that museums should serve a wide public in inventive ways has provided livelier exhibit techniques and exhibitions; a new, imaginative use of the Mall through such events as the annual Festival of American Folklife, and a greatly expanded range of activities that has brought into being such units as the Anacostia Neighborhood Museum, the Smithsonian Associates, the Division of Performing Arts, and the Renwick Gallery.

Focal point of this world of scholarly activity, with a distinguished history of its own since 1849 is

The Smithsonian Institution Building

The Smithsonian's "Castle on the Mall" was designed in the Norman style of architecture by James Renwick, Jr., who designed Grace Church and St. Patrick's Cathedral in New York City. He also designed the Renwick Gallery, described on page 119. Built of red sandstone from nearby Seneca Creek, Maryland, the Castle consists of a central section and two wings joined to it by connecting ranges. It is 447 feet long and has a maximum depth of 160 feet. Its eight crenelated towers, the highest standing 146 feet, make it a distinctive landmark on the Mall.

The cornerstone was laid in May 1847 at a gala public ceremony. Although the building was not completed until 1855, it was partially occupied in 1849 when the east wing was opened for the Secretary and his staff and for public lectures. During the Smithsonian's early years the building housed all operations of the Institution. It contained a science museum, a lecture hall, an art gallery, research laboratories, administrative offices, and living quarters for the Secretary and his family.

Major reconstruction was undertaken following a fire that destroyed the upper part of the main building and the north and south towers in January 1865. The east wing was enlarged in 1883. In recent years the interior of the central section has been reconstructed to provide additional administrative offices, and the whole building is being provided with original furnishings reflecting the taste of the Victorian era that produced the structure.

Today the Secretary's and other administrative offices occupy the east wing. Other parts of the upper floors also house a library and offices for visiting scholars.

Open to the public, the Great Hall on the ground floor contains exhibits relating to the history of the Institution and its Secretaries. The Reception Center for Smithsonian Associates is behind it; in the west wing are the Smithsonian Archives and the Smithsonian Commons. The tomb of founder James Smithson is located in the north foyer.

Engraving of the Smithsonian Institution Building during the mid-19th century.

(RIGHT) Decorated ice delivery wagon from the turn of the century.

(OPPOSITE PAGE) Carrousel animal.

Model Beam-type engine, 1838.

Political parade.

The National Museum of History and Technology

BROOKE HINDLE, Director

Mall entrance: North side between 12th and 14th Streets, N.W.
Constitution Avenue entrance: Between 12th and 14th Streets, N.W.
Open: Daily except Christmas
Hours: 10:00 a.m. to 5:30 p.m. (later in summer)
Telephone: (202) 381-6264

What's going on and where to find it

Information Desks
Located near the Mall and Constitution Avenue entrances, with up-to-date information on special events, seminars, films, and other activities. Phone: 381-6264

Topical Exhibits
Announcements of current exhibits of special interest are posted on all floors.

Guided Tours
Guided Tours for school groups and *Highlight Tours.* Must be scheduled two weeks in advance. Drop-in tours also available. Phone: 381-6471

Cafeteria and Snack Bar
Located at the west end of the basement level. Open daily from 10:00 a.m. to 5:00 p.m. (later in summer).

The Smithsonian Bookstore—a McGraw-Hill Enterprise
Located to the right of the Constitution Avenue entrance. The largest museum bookshop in the world, more than 10,000 titles are devoted to all aspects of Americana.

Museum Shops
At three locations: to the left of the Mall entrance, on the First Floor directly below it, and to the left of the Constitution Avenue entrance. Postcards, slides, jewelry, games, and museum-related objects are for sale.

Smithsonian Station
A 19th-century country-store post office operated by the U.S. Postal Service next to the Constitution Avenue entrance. Provides full postal service except parcel post and money orders.

The First Ladies Hall.

Printing press similar to the one used by Benjamin Franklin.

A different kind of museum . . .

This magnificent modern building belies all the old fashioned concepts of museums as dusty depositories of curios and relics of interest only to the specialist. Here, in hall after memorable hall, is the history of America's genius—in its people, and in its technology, industry, craftsmanship, and design.

The original Star-Spangled Banner, the First Ladies' gowns, Ben Franklin's printing press, Edison's electric lamp are some of the singular treasures. But there is more, much more—to look at, to listen to, and, even, to smell. For this is a museum to have fun in, and that is best attested to by the more than six million visitors who come each year from all parts of the world to experience some of the excitement and grandeur of the American heritage.

Enter the museum from the Mall side and you encounter the original *Star-Spangled Banner,* hanging in tattered grandeur. This is the historic flag that flew over Fort McHenry during the successful defense against the British fleet on September 13, 1814. Next morning, on seeing that "the flag was still there," a Baltimore lawyer named Francis Scott Key was inspired to write the words of the poem that, set to the music of an earlier tune, became the national anthem of the United States. Sewn by a Baltimore widow, Mary Pickersgill, the flag was in keeping with the new nation's defiant mood in the War of 1812—big and bold, with a star and a stripe for each member state of the Union at the time. It is presently displayed against a backing fabric that shows its original size—30 feet high and

The Star-Spangled Banner.

Interior of the reconstructed country-store, post office.

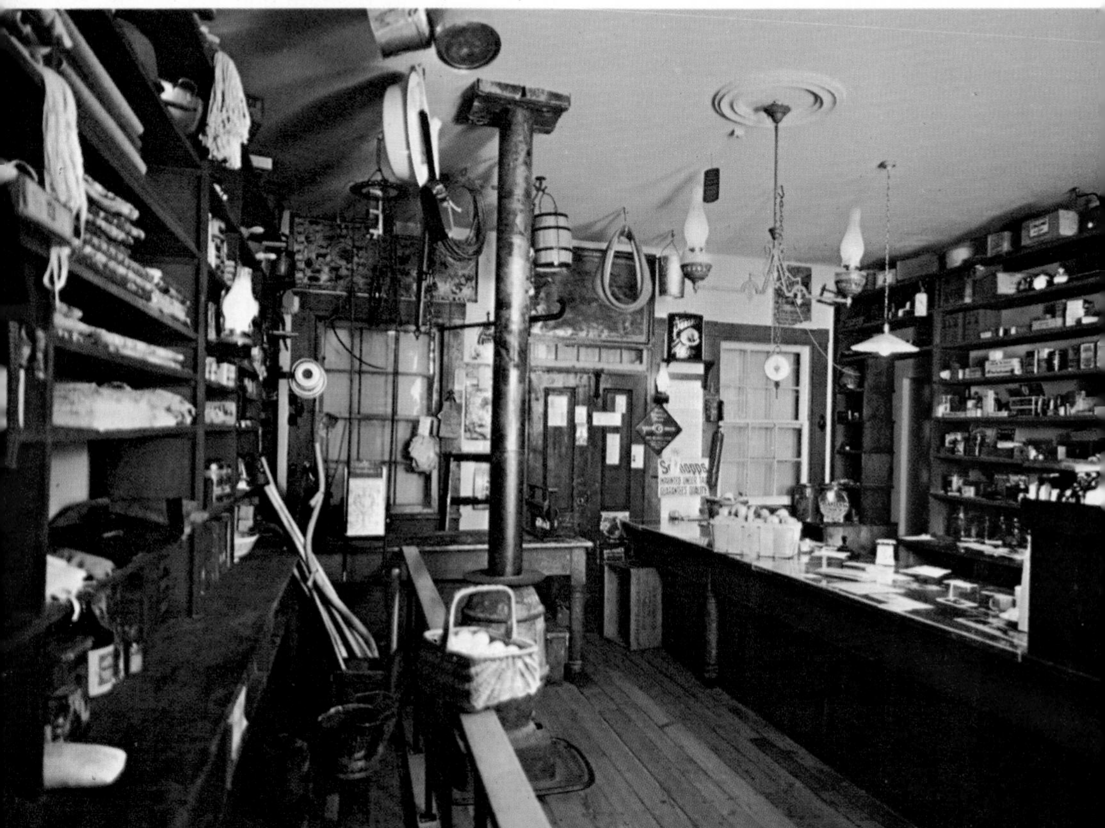

42 feet from side to side. The missing portion was cut off piecemeal as souvenirs before there was a law against mutilation of the American flag.

Enter the museum from the Constitution Avenue side and you will find, to your left, a genuine country-store post office. Step inside to browse among the staples and sundries that typify this uniquely American merchandising phenomenon. This store existed in Headsville, West Virginia, and was engaged in active business between 1861 and 1914. Its removal, "lock, stock, and barrel," to the Smithsonian in 1971 and its authorization as a U.S. Postal Service substation, selling stamps and forwarding mail, entitles it to the postmark, *Smithsonian Station.*

From either entry, go to the center of the building to observe the remarkable *Foucault Pendulum*, which demonstrates the rotation of the earth. Suspended a length of 71½ feet from the fourth-floor ceiling, it swings to and fro over a marble pattern of a mariner's compass rose on which red markers are arranged in a circle. One by one, as the day passes, the pendulum knocks down the markers. Although the pendulum seems to change its path, it is actually the floor beneath it that is carried around by the daily rotation of the earth while the pendulum continues to swing stably in space. This, the first satisfactory method of showing the earth's rotation, was demonstrated by the French physicist Leon Foucault in 1851, more than 300 years after Copernicus, the founder of modern astronomy, had proposed the daily rotation of the earth on theoretical grounds.

Foucault Pendulum.

Finding your way around . . .

This is a huge museum, and its flow of exhibit areas carries you from one fascinating subject to another. We suggest that you keep the following floor plans handy; orient yourself to the east and west sides of the building by establishing which is on your left and which on your right— and start looking!

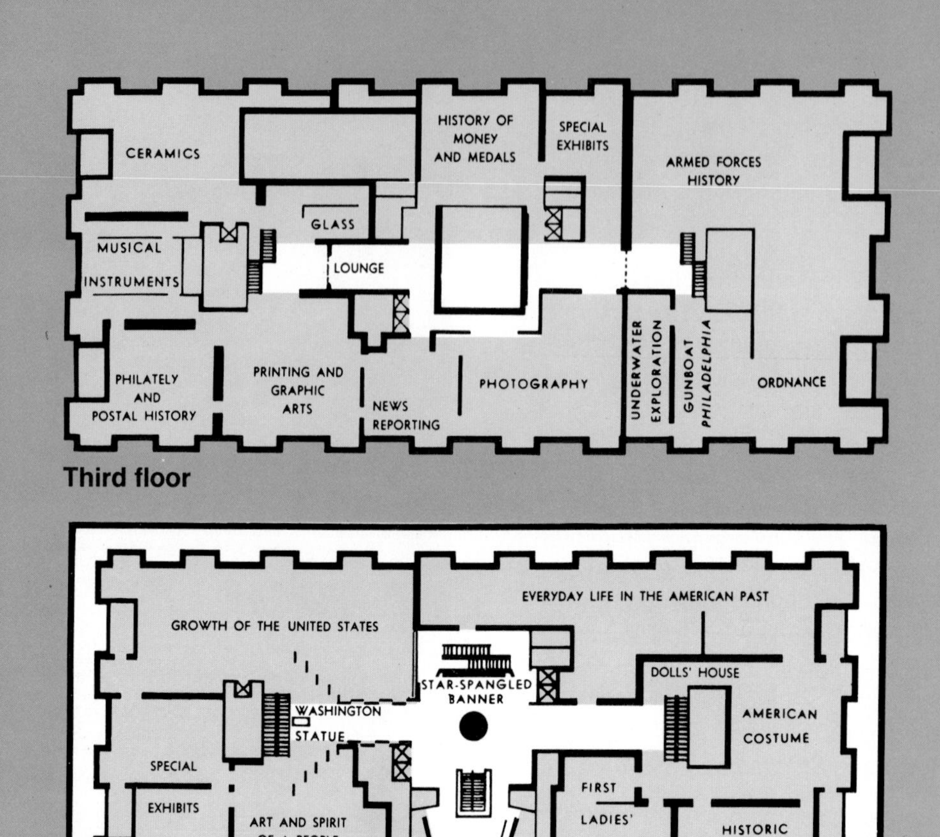

Third floor

Second floor

THE MALL

CONSTITUTION AVENUE

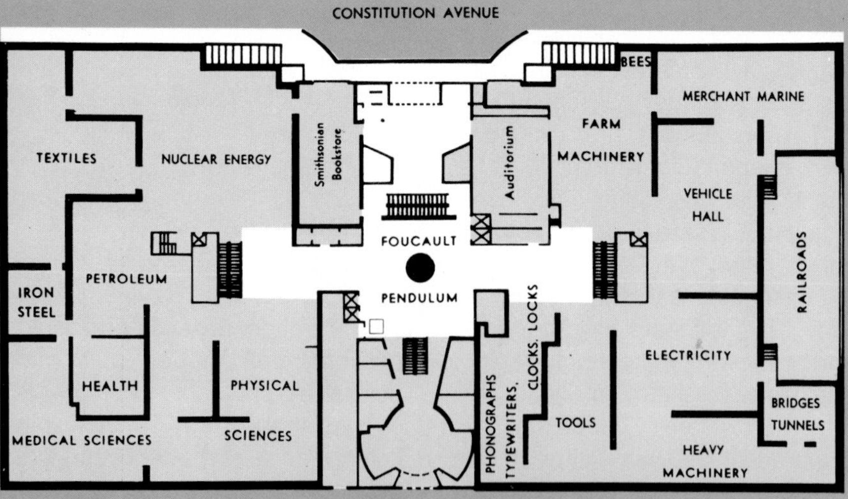

First floor

THE NATIONAL MUSEUM OF HISTORY AND TECHNOLOGY

FIRST FLOOR—EAST

Farm Machinery

Here is dramatic witness of the extent to which mechanized equipment has supplanted the simple hand tools of the 18th and early 19th-century farmer. Compare a wooden plow of colonial times with the tractor-powered gang plow; the traditional cradle scythe, flail, and winnowing fan with a 20-mule-team Holt combine of 1886. The McCormack-Deering cotton harvester was the first of the mechanical cotton pickers that revolutionized southern agriculture and influenced urban migrations.

Early steam and kerosene powered tractors, and an extensive collection of scale models illustrate the implements and methods of agriculture through the years.

Behind this hall, a seasonal attraction is an observational beehive with 60,000 active inhabitants.

Vehicles

From a "one-hoss shay" to a "merry Oldsmobile," the Smithsonian's exhibition of horse-drawn and motor powered vehicles tells the story of America's progress on the road. The museum draws from time to time on its collection of more than forty rare masterpieces of antique auto artistry

Water-powered sawmill, 18th and 19th centuries, eastern Pennsylvania.

Scale model of the 1901 Huber steam traction engine.

Winton Bullet No. 2, 1902.

to show such unique examples as the first Duryea (1893) and the first Haynes (1894); a 1903 Oldsmobile and a 1913 Ford Model-T; early racing cars like Barney Oldfield's Winton Bullet (1902); a White motorbus (1917); and a variety of fire engines and trucks.

Back to horses: there are a chaise from 1770 and carriages—some elegant and some utilitarian—complete with sound effects.

Among the earliest cycles is a Draisine, or hobbyhorse, from 1818. Others range through the whole 19th century and on to today's modern 10-speed bike.

American Merchant Shipping

Ship models—most of them built to scale from original plans, and many of them historic—fire the imagination of any Sunday sailor. In the wake of a 9th-century Viking ship, the models are arranged to illustrate the changes that have taken place in the American merchant marine since earliest colonial times. Here are the *Santa Maria,* the *Mayflower,* and great ocean liners such as the *Santa Rosa* and

Rigged model of a typical New Haven oyster boat.

Model of an 1873 steam fire engine.

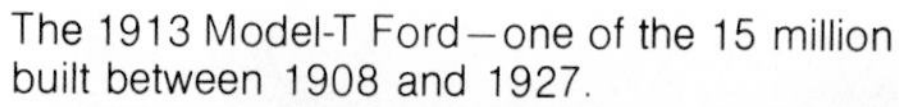

The 1913 Model-T Ford—one of the 15 million built between 1908 and 1927.

Independence, along with ocean freighters, lake ore carriers, and specialized craft. Centrally located are the fast clipper ships that dominated the sea-lanes until the 19th century. There are early steamers, fishing boats, and a profusion of smaller craft—ferries, tugs, and work boats. Other exhibits deal with ship design, navigation instruments, sailmaking, and the skills and crafts required aboard ship.

(For models of ships of war, exhibited in the Armed Forces Hall, see p. 42.)

Model stern-wheel towboat, 1924.

Steam passenger locomotive No. 1401 built for the Southern Railway in 1926.

Railroads

Come upon this vast area and listen to the sounds that mean "All Aboard!" The raucous hoots of the chime whistle of a modern steam locomotive, the syncopated chug as it gathers speed, the deafening roar of the powerful engine thundering down the tracks, the rhythmic clangs of the crossing signals—these sounds are typical of the great Southern Railway's Pacific-type passenger engine, the gigantic 1401 that dominates the hall.

Contrast this with the Pioneer, a 12½-ton engine built in 1851 that served for nearly forty years on the Cumberland Valley Railroad. Designed to show the development of railroading, with emphasis on typical or standard equipment, this hall is one of the museum's most popular. At one end is a full-size cable car of 1888 from Seattle shown on a cutaway section of cable-railway track. Nearby are a diorama of New York's Third Avenue Elevated as it looked in 1880, and Moses Farmer's small electric locomotive of 1847.

Pioneer passenger locomotive, 1851.

At the opposite end is a full-size eight-wheel passenger car, from 1836, the oldest in existence. Many scale models show the development of passenger cars, locomotives, and freight cars from the early 18th century. Throughout the hall are other exhibits that demonstrate the development of air brakes, couplers, automatic signaling devices, and rails.

Civil Engineering

Bridge and tunnel constructions from the Roman era to the present are shown in detailed displays. Three major timbering systems used in mid-19th-century tunnels are reconstructed to scale. Models of famous bridges, including a series of Roebling's Brooklyn Bridge (1870s), show how various types—arch, truss, cantilever, suspension—are built. Eight large models illustrate the advance of tunneling technology.

Power Machinery

Power-producing machinery, which provided the muscle of the industrial age, occupies this hall. Full-size engines, illustrations, and working models describe the attempts to harness atmospheric force (1660-1700); the early age of steam power (1700-1770); and the development of high-pressure and high-speed engines (1800-1920). The development of steam boilers and the steam turbine is also traced. Another section of the hall shows the use of water power from the water wheel in a simple water mill to huge modern hydroelectric turbines. A group of original gas and liquid-fueled engines are exhibited, tracing the historical development of the internal combustion prime mover. Some of the machines are enormous; many had been producing industrial power for decades when retired from service. A number of the models in the hall are operative, awaiting the push of a button to explain the functioning of the originals which tower over them.

Electricity

A complete presentation of the historic development of the various concepts, theories, and applications of electricity is the theme of this hall. It begins with five concepts developed prior to the mid-19th century: electricity and matter; electricity and chemistry; electricity and magnetism; electricity and heat; electricity and physiology. The various forms of electricity resulted in numerous unrelated theories on the nature of electric phenomena, including Benjamin Franklin's significant contribution in this field. An 18th-century "scientific" parlor game is shown in a life-size working tableau, which shows a lady being given an "electric kiss" by a gentleman. This utilizes a large electrostatic apparatus.

During the latter part of the 19th century the synthesis of the early

Mill engine (1852) used to turn a machine shop.

Entrance to the Civil Engineering Hall.

(LEFT) One segment of the model showing the construction of the Brooklyn Bridge.

Riedler pumping engine, driven by Pelton turbine, 1901.

A demonstration in the Machine Shop (1830-1855).

Principle of electricity illustrated in the "electric kiss".

concepts was accomplished in the work of scientists such as Henry, Weber, Faraday, Maxwell, and Hertz, whose individual contributions are explained.

Recent scientific applications are shown in working demonstration models of laser and maser beams and the making of a hologram. The generation, measurement, and use of electric power in our lives is shown in a special section devoted to electric communications—the telegraph, telephone, and radio. Among the exhibits are Alexander Graham Bell's early telephone and Edwin H. Armstrong's crucial contributions to the growth of radio. Recent developments in radar and radio astronomy are included.

A small up-to-date library and reading room are an integral part of the hall.

Tools

The throb of heavy machinery at work is often heard here as periodic demonstrations suggest factories in mass-production. A fully equipped mid-19th-century machine shop contrasts with historic examples of Roman and Renaissance implements and industrial hand tools of the last century. A 1905 multiple spindle drill or a series in automatic sequence like the automatic screw machine of 1888 are actually run during demonstration times. Nearby are exhibits explaining the operation of such basic tools as the lathe, shaper, grinder, and milling machine, and examples of the measuring devices used to achieve the precision needed in the manufacture of standardized machine parts.

Pocket watch, Howard, Davis and Dennison, Roxbury, Massachusetts, 1852.

Phonographs, Typewriters, Clocks, Locks

Here are timekeepers of all kinds; record players; typewriters; and, tucked away in one corner, locks. From sundials and waterclocks, methods of measuring time are displayed in a rare sequence of their development. There are splendid examples of mechanical clocks dating from the 14th century; a variety of astronomical clocks, and incredibly accurate electronic and, even, atomic "clocks." The sound-recording section contains such early epoch-making inventions as Edison's first phonograph of 1877, Berliner's Gramophone of 1888, and the Victor Talking Machine. Almost entirely an American achievement, the typewriter is exhibited in various stages of progress from its beginnings with an 1829 patent.

FIRST FLOOR—WEST

Physical Sciences and Mathematics

Here are the instruments and apparatuses man has devised to explore, measure, and comprehend his environment. Within a reproduction of a 2nd-century Greek courtyard is a seated figure using an astronomical instrument of that time. Jesse Ramsden's famous dividing engine of the 1770s is nearby, along with a replica of Tycho Brahe's great equatorial armillary of the 16th century. A varied collection of smaller instruments from 1150 to 1800 exemplifies the art of their makers. Beyond are exhibits that recall the teaching of science in the early 19th century and a panoramic

Astronomical instruments of the 2nd century.

(TOP) Diorama showing Benjamin Banneker and Andrew Ellicott laying out the nation's capital, 1791.

(CENTER) Workshop of the telescope maker, Henry Fitz, circa 1850.

(BOTTOM) Interior of an American pharmacy during the 1880s.

view of the surveying of the District of Columbia by Andrew Ellicott and Benjamin Banneker.

A mathematical section presents adding and calculating machines, slide rules, early automatic computers, and other data processing devices.

To see what 19th-century astronomy was like, view the observatory and the telescope-making shop of Henry Fitz.

A chemistry laboratory of the late 18th century, equipped with glassware used by Joseph Priestly is in marked contrast to the more modern laboratory of the 1880s.

Medical Sciences and Health

A transparent mannequin in the *Hall of Health* shows the important organs of the body. Other displays feature methods of plastic surgery and basic physiological processes such as the growth of a foetus.

George Washington's false teeth, made of gold and ivory, occupy a place of prominence in the *Hall of Dentistry* which also contains two reconstructed dental offices and a laboratory of the 1900s.

Displays in the *Hall of Pharmacy* are a far cry from today's super drug store. See the delightful 18th-century European apothecary shop with its elegant collection of drug jars and an American pharmacy of 1890, completely equipped. Adjacent exhibits help to explain the origin of drugs, the tools of the apothecary, and recent developments in antibiotics.

The *Hall of Medicine* traces the evolution of healing from its beginnings in magic and superstition to modern cardiac and bone surgery. A

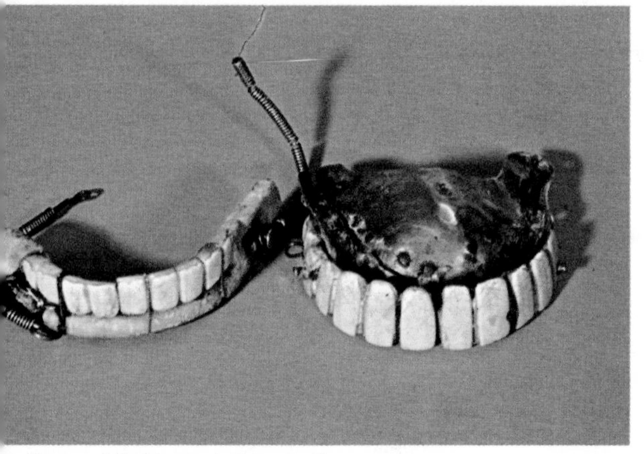

George Washington's false teeth.

(TOP RIGHT) Model rigs in the Petroleum Hall.

(RIGHT) Drill rig used at Spindletop, Texas, oilfield, 1901.

reconstructed room from Boston's Massachusetts General Hospital as it appeared in the late 1870s contains original furnishings. The earliest anaesthetic equipment (1840s), a biological laboratory of 1850, one of the first iron lungs, and a pioneer mechanical heart are among the wide aspect of medicine covered by other exhibits in the halls.

Iron and Steel

One large model shows the complex operation of a modern steel mill. Others show the open-hearth and basic-oxygen processes of making steel; how a colonial iron smelter operated in 1650; and methods of applying protective coatings of tin and ceramics to steel. Among historic objects is a Bessemer-type converter of 1862.

Petroleum

A 57-foot panoramic mural at the entrance shows important aspects of the history and technology of the petroleum industry. You are able to see the geologic conditions under which oil is found; methods of discovering, drilling, recovering, transporting, and refining; and the significance of the petrochemical industries. Actual equipment on display includes an original rotary drill (1902-type); the original Burton-Humphries and Cross experimental stills for "cracking" or refining petroleum; and a variety of well-head equipment, like the "Christmas-tree" used to control the flow of oil.

Textiles

Today's devotees of spinning and weaving may step back in time to see the origins of their avocations. Here are historic examples of carding, spinning, and weaving machines of the kind that moved textile-making from a family operation at home to an industry employing thousands of workers in factories. The machines include Samuel Slater's spinning frame of 1790 and a Jacquard loom of 1840. Exhibits of embroidery and needlework show examples of these household arts, and periodic demonstrations explain the techniques of hand-spinning and weaving.

Nuclear Energy

Important milestones in the exploration and taming of nuclear energy are represented by original apparatus. The Dunning cyclotron was used by John R. Dunning of Columbia University in 1941 to split the atomic nucleus for the first time in the United States. This showed that uranium-235, a rare isotope, was the most readily fissionable component of natural uranium. Further experiments led to the achievement of controlled nuclear fission. A full-size cutaway replica of the world's first atomic pile, in which such a controlled, self-sustaining chain reaction was achieved, stands in the hall. The original was built by Enrico Fermi and his team of scientists at the University of Chicago where the historic event took place on December 2, 1942.

Other important pieces of nuclear research hardware on view are the Tuve-Van de Graaf particle accelerator of 1931 and a full-size

demonstration model of the Figure-8 "stellarator," which Spitzer used at Princeton in 1951 in an important experiment toward controlled nuclear fusion.

SECOND FLOOR—CENTER OF BUILDING AND EAST

Everyday Life in the American Past

This, one of the liveliest areas in the museum, is exactly what it says it is—an incomparable insight into the ways Americans have been living for three hundred years. The chronological display begins at the hall entrance directly behind the Star-Spangled Banner. Here are authentic house interiors and original objects related to the diverse sources of our culture. Our European heritage is depicted in ten room settings showing typical living quarters from such far-flung areas as New Mexico, Quebec, Virginia, and California. The earliest is

(LEFT) Petit-point depiction of *The Queen of Sheba Admiring the Wisdom of Solomon,* made in 1744.

(BELOW) Princeton stellarator (left) and Tuve-Van de Graaf particle accelerator.

(ABOVE LEFT) California ranch kitchen of the 1860s.

(ABOVE RIGHT) Jacquard loom showing use of punched cards to weave pattern.

(LEFT) One-room school of the 1860s.

Metal toy with movable parts.

(TOP, OPPOSITE PAGE) View of the *Hall of Historic Americans* showing a political parade.

(BOTTOM LEFT, OPPOSITE PAGE) The desk on which Thomas Jefferson wrote the Declaration of Independence, 1776.

(BOTTOM RIGHT, OPPOSITE PAGE) The suit worn by Abraham Lincoln during the last day of his life.

a second-floor sleeping chamber from the house of Seth Story, a farmer of Essex, Massachusetts, built in about 1680. There are a California ranch kitchen; a Colonial parlor; a Victorian library; a 1915 suburban dining room. Among other settings, see how children studied in a one-room New England schoolhouse of 1863; smell a Georgetown confectionary shop of 1900. Complete architectural models include a Delaware log house of about 1740 and a Maryland tenant farmer's house from 1880. Intermingled in the displays are tools, household utensils, tableware, silver, pewter, games and toys, books, folk art, and "homely objects."

American Costume

Hard to imagine the styles of the seventies—jeans and beads— in here some day? Maybe. But from the early 1700s Americans have been fashion conscious, and this beautifully preserved collection moves gracefully

Exhibit showing the style of clothing in 1929.

through the changes of the centuries —right up to the "little black dress." Colonial gowns, the Empire and Victorian lines, the opulence of the Gay Nineties, and the daring chic of the Flapper are depicted in authentic settings. Accompanying the chronological order of the garments are appropriate accessories of the times—shawls, gloves, shoes, hats, and a few fabulous diamond and emerald baubles that always have been just the right finishing touch.

Historic Americans

Seventy-six trombones—or thereabouts—greet you as you come upon this panorama of electioneering America. The evolution of political campaigning through the 19th, and into the 20th century comes to life before your eyes with the music, banners, buttons, and other devices that mean so much to American political history. Elsewhere in the hall are campaign objects and personal memorabilia of individuals who have contributed to U.S. history in government and politics. Here are the desk upon which Thomas Jefferson drafted the Declaration of Independence; possessions of the Washington and Adams families; the "business" suit worn by Abraham Lincoln on the last day of his life.

Among the furnishings is the "Resolute" desk presented to President Rutherford B. Hayes in 1878 by Queen Victoria. The desk remained in the White House and was used by every President from the time of Hayes through the administration of John F. Kennedy.

Gowns worn by First Ladies, Claudia Taylor Johnson, Jacqueline Kennedy and Mamie Eisenhower to the Inaugural Balls for their husbands.

First Ladies

From the pink ribbed silk of Martha Washington to the mimosa silk satin of Pat Nixon, gowns of the First Ladies—wives, daughters, or official hostesses of the United States—are shown in elegant tableaux featuring period settings similar to the surroundings in which they were originally worn. These authentic gowns are a treasure of styling changes of the past two centuries. This representation, unique to The National Museum of History and Technology, is certainly one of the most appealing to Smithsonian visitors.

Displayed in special vitrines is an incomparable sampling of *White House China,* showing plates and other table china used for state occasions since the early days of the Republic. The collection begins with the service the Washington family used in their various official residences. Almost every administration added its own different set, many of which, during the first half of the 19th century, were of French manufacture. During this century equally beautiful American designs prevail. The exhibition also includes some pieces of the spectacular china used at present-day state dinners.

(TOP LEFT) Working model of Eli Whitney's cotton gin.

(TOP RIGHT) Uniform and sword worn by General George Washington, 1783.

(BELOW) Conestoga Wagon 1840s.

SECOND FLOOR—WEST

The Growth of the United States 1640-1750 — 1750-1851

In two centuries America grew from a raw wilderness to a vigorous nation. These two adjoining exhibition areas highlight objects from these two centuries of American experience covering, to mention only a few aspects, education, religion, money and finance, communication, law and government, architecture, transportation, arts and crafts, industrial technology. These composite halls serve as a basic guide to the whole museum and other important collections of the Smithsonian. Included among the diversified artifacts are an English printing press, typical of those on which Benjamin Franklin labored as a journeyman printer in London in 1726; a uniform worn by George Washington; the engine and boiler of John Steven's 1804 steamboat; a six-horse Conestoga wagon; an electromagnet devised in 1831 by Joseph Henry; and a reconstructed framework of a Massachusetts house showing building methods of the 17th and 18th centuries.

Horatio Greenough's statue of George Washington.

Statue of George Washington

This heroic-sized statue by Boston-born Horatio Greenough, who is considered the first important American sculptor, exemplifies the classical revival in the United States after the Revolutionary War.

The Congress commissioned Greenough to create the statue in 1832. Working in Italy the artist completed the work in 1840. The likeness is based on Jean Antoine Houdon's *George Washington* at the Virginia state capitol, while the torso and the pose is from the ancient Greek *Zeus* by Phidias.

Sent to the United States in 1841 it stood in the rotunda of the Capitol for two years when it was moved to the Capitol grounds. In 1908 it was transferred to the Smithsonian Institution. Seeing the "Father of Our Country" portrayed in classical attire was never quite appreciated in spite of the noble allusions to Greek antiquity.

(BOTTOM OF PAGE) *Winter Scene.* After a lithograph published by Nathaniel Currier, New York, 1853.

(LEFT) Weather vane—*Gabriel.* Copyright by L. W. Cushing & Sons, Waltham, Mass., 1883.

(ABOVE) Painted wooden Indian squaw, probably used to attract customers to tobacconist's shop, late 19th century.

(LEFT AND BELOW) Carrousel animals.

Art and Spirit of a People

You can't ride the carrousel horse or lion, but here stand splendid examples of two centuries of popular and folk art. With merry-go-round music in the background, delight in the Van Alstyne collection of Americana. Recalling the arts and crafts of yesteryear, now being revived, the exhibit features a cigar store Indian, weather vanes, paintings, objects in wood and metal, and needlework.

THIRD FLOOR—EAST

Armed Forces History

Uniforms, weapons and equipment, flags, and models of naval vessels illustrate the origin and growth of the armed forces through westward explorations to the First and Second World Wars. A special highlight is the field headquarters tent and personal gear of General George Washington. Another is an intact Revolutionary War vessel—the Continental gunboat *Philadelphia*, the oldest American man-of-war in existence. Built in 1776 and sunk in battle on Lake Champlain the same year, she was recovered in 1935 with much of her equipment. Other important ship models are John Paul Jones' flagship and the frigate *Constellation* of 1797. The Civil War is reflected in models of Union and Confederate Ironclads. World War II ships and later developments are displayed in large-scale models, among them the U.S.S. *Missouri* on which Japan signed the formal surrender documents ending the Second World War.

Revolutionary War gunboat *Philadelphia,* sunk in Lake Champlain, 1776.

Camp chest used by George Washington during the Revolution.

Ordnance

The development of weapons from the Stone Age to modern times is shown in dramatic fashion. From the Museum's extensive collection of small arms are works—including, in some instances, the inventor's patent model—of such notable gunmakers as Colt (six-shot revolver and first Colt hand gun of 1836); Remington (rifle); and Browning (machine gun). The Gatling gun, the first practical

American Gatling battery gun, 1862.

machine gun (1862) is displayed, as are models of heavy ordnance such as railway guns, armored vehicles and tanks, and missile launchers. Other exhibits illustrate the development of mass production in arms, making through the introduction of interchangeable parts, and explain the mechanisms, components, and operation of weapons and weapons systems.

Underwater Exploration

"The sea is giving up its secrets . . ." declares the opening description to the Hall's disclosures of modern scientific methods of recovering historic treasures from ships sunk centuries ago. The underwater archeologist at work is shown in a life-size exhibit—the focal point for the exciting examples of diving gear used in investigating the seabed and actual finds such as cannons, tools, coins, and other treasures.

Photography

The nation's millions of camera fans have a chance to have some fun amidst this panoramic assemblage of the equipment and materials of the art of photography. Here, period settings show the first darkroom; one of the first photojournalists—Roger Fenton—documenting the Crimean War; an early studio; an explorer-photographer; and other historic scenes. You can operate early penny arcade equipment and have your portrait taken with the tintype process. A large array of early photographs and still and motion picture equipment is displayed. A special gallery features a changing print program.

View of the Hall of Underwater Exploration.

History of Money and Medals

For the youngest collector or the most sophisticated numismatist there is something of interest in this sweeping look at monetary tokens of the centuries. The evolution of monetary exchange from primitive barter with seashells, beads, stones, and furs to our modern, complex economy is detailed with examples of metallic coins, paper notes, tokens, and related objects. Features are the breathtaking Gold Room, containing much of the Josiah K. Lilly collection of gold coins, the oldest of which dates from the 7th century B.C.; the collectors' browsing area, with a series of U.S. coins; an imaginative children's corner; exhibits of historic and classic forgeries, and periodic demonstrations of coin-stamping machines and presses.

THIRD FLOOR—WEST

The Henry R. Luce Hall of News Reporting

The history of American news reporting, from the 17th century to today, is demonstrated through the extraordinary changes that have occurred in communications technology. Newsreels, television sets, radios, teletype machines, telegraph keys, space satellites, and a special Apollo 11 moon camera are in continuous operation. Rare newspapers, still photographs, and prints, as well as slide presentations, are also exhibited. All aim to illustrate the impact of technological invention on both the style and the meaning of news.

The 1804 silver dollar is a publicized rarity in the United States coin series.

Athenian four drachma silver coin from the 5th century B.C.

(LEFT) A 100-ducat piece from Prague (left) and a 1/32 ducat piece from Regensburg in Germany representing the largest and smallest coins ever struck.

Printing and Graphic Arts

The marvels of printing techniques—from a Rembrandt etching to a modern newspaper—are shown in a progression of displays that highlight the wide range of mechanical reproduction through the ages.

Japanese printmaking.

(LEFT) Columbian, 1865, first American iron printing press.

Artistry and ingenuity as developed by the Japanese in their woodcut prints of the last century are depicted in a life-size setting of a workshop, with authentic equipment and costumes. Demonstration shops show a hand-press of the 1750s; a job-printing press of a century later; a steam-powered newspaper press of the 1880s. A type foundry, offset and etching presses, and typesetting machines show advancements made in the profession up to today's remarkable computerized typesetting machines.

(ABOVE) The exterior of a replica of Benjamin Franklin's printing shop —post office.

(RIGHT) First American postal issue, 1847.

(FAR RIGHT) The most celebrated rarity among U.S. postal issues, printed in 1918.

Stamps and the Mails

Even if you've never been a stamp collector you will enjoy this survey of the whole history of the movement of written communication. Although the exhibition begins with clay tablets and papyrus letters, the emphasis is on the development within the United States of a postal system that could keep pace with the demands of a fast growing population spreading westward. Models showing types of vehicles used, from two-wheel carts to the airplane, parallel the progress of the mails from George Washington's time (one of his letters is here) through the pony express and the important innovation of Rural Free Delivery to the 20th century's delivery system. Machines of all kinds demonstrate mail-handling methods and the production of postage stamps.

For the philatelist—amateur or professional—there is real excitement in the magnificent National Postage Stamp Collection that is represented by more than 75,000 stamps—both domestic and foreign—in pullout frames for closer viewing.

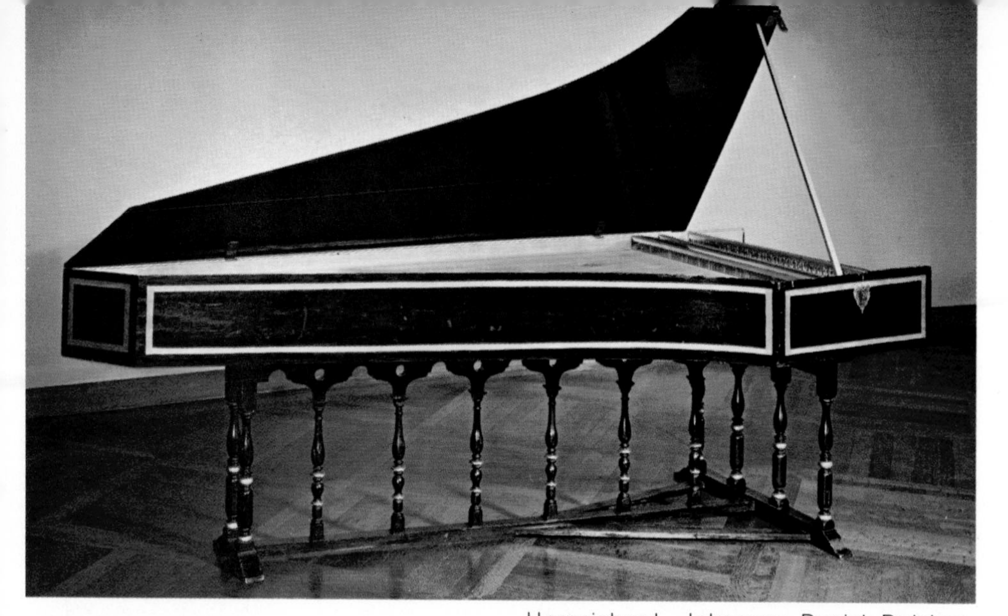

Harpsichord, Johannes Daniel Dulcken, Antwerp, 1745.

Demonstration area in the Hall of Musical Instruments.

Musical Instruments

In a charming setting that includes a chamber-music hall frequently used for concerts are some exquisite examples of European musical instruments from the 17th and 18th centuries, as well as later American instruments. Carefully restored to playing condition in the Smithsonian's workshop, these range from harpsichords and organs to banjos and dulcimers. Relax in one of four "stereophonic chairs" and listen to music recorded on antique instruments from the collection, and observe the slide-and-sound documentary on Appalachian folk music which supplements another part of the exhibit.

Ceramics

The potter in action is seen in a documentary film that introduces the several galleries comprising this remarkable and very large collection of antique ceramics from Europe, the Orient, and the United States. Eighteenth-century porcelain from the Syz collection; the Larsen and McCauley collections of English earthenwares decorated with views of America; the Wires collection of ceramic tiles; the Leon collection of yellow-glazed English earthenware lead to the final gallery devoted to American ceramics and the work of contemporary studio potters.

(ABOVE LEFT) American art pottery. Late 19th and early 20th-centuries.

(ABOVE RIGHT) Glass jar and cover possibly made in the Pittsburgh, Pennsylvania area, 19th century.

(LEFT) French paper weights, 19th century.

Glass

Illuminated alcoves highlight the beauty of the collection that traces the development of glass making, with exhibits that illustrate design and production techniques of various civilizations and cultures. Some of the earliest known glass objects from Egypt, Roman glass, and later European examples are displayed, as are rare paperweights from France and the United States. There are lead and cut crystal from England; American 18th-century Stiegel and Amelung; 19th-century Tiffany. The queen of 20th-century production —Steuben—is shown in several exquisite examples, along with contemporary Swedish and European works.

History and Growth of the Collections

Back in 1858 the "objects of art and of foreign and curious research" in the National Cabinet of Curiosities were transferred from the Patent Office to the Smithsonian by Congressional order. This was the origin of what is now The National Museum of History and Technology. Then, in 1876, a windfall in the form of articles displayed at the Philadelphia Centennial Exposition—some forty freight-car loads in all—was turned over to the Smithsonian.

Over the past century these collections have expanded to more than 14,000,000 items. Many come from government agencies as, for example, samples of all stamps turned out by the U.S. Treasury's Bureau of Engraving and Printing and coins issued by the U. S. Mint. Twice since 1900 the Commerce Department has contributed extensive collections of patent models of inventions, including Howe's sewing machine and Edison's phonograph. But most of the objects are the gifts of individuals, or private and public institutions, or foreign countries wishing to express gratitude to a nation that has offered opportunity and friendship.

Those objects for which space was available were displayed in the Arts and Industries Building and earned the Smithsonian the name, "the Nation's Attic." Between the 1880s and 1964, visitors crowded its halls and corridors and delighted in its treasures.

Today the style is different. The spacious halls of The National Museum of History and Technology are filled with color and the exhibits—dramatically, beautifully mounted—present the rarities and wonders of the nation's experience.

Building

Authorized by Congress in 1954, The National Museum of History and Technology was designed in a modified classical style by the New York firm of McKim, Mead & White. Groundbreaking ceremonies took place in 1958; the cornerstone was laid in 1961; and the building opened to the public in January 1964.

The museum measures 578 by 302 feet and is 121 feet high. It is faced with rose-white Tennessee marble. Three of its five floors are devoted to public exhibits. Curators' offices, laboratories and storage areas occupy the upper two floors. Workshops and service facilities are in the basement, along with a special exhibit hall and a public cafeteria which overlooks a sunken garden with a view of the Washington Monument.

A handsome forty-foot jet black steel stabile by Alexander Calder rests in a reflecting pool at the edge of the garden. At the Mall entrance the sensitive stainless steel sculpture, *Infinity*, by American artist José de Rivera, turns almost imperceptibly atop its obelisk-shaped pedestal.

Infinity by José de Rivera

(ABOVE) A diorama depicting the dinosaur *Triceratops*

(RIGHT) A Chinese opera (detail).

(OPPOSITE PAGE)
Millerite specimen with free standing crystal spray.

National Museum of Natural History

PORTER M. KIER, Director

Mall entrance: North side at 10th St., N.W.
Constitution Avenue entrance: at 10th St., N.W.
Open: Daily except Christmas
Hours: 10:00 a.m. to 5:30 p.m. (later in summer)
Telephone: (202) 381-6264

What's going on and where to find it

Information Desks
Located near the Mall and Constitution Avenue entrances, with up-to-date information on special events, lectures, seminars, films, and other activities.

By-Word
Headsets for a sound-guided tour of the exhibits are available for rent at desks near the entrances.

Guided Tours
Guided School Tours and *Weekend Highlight Tours* must be scheduled two weeks in advance.

Museum Shops
To right of Mall entrance, and inside Constitution Avenue entrance. Books and booklets emphasizing natural history subjects; postcards and slides; jewelry; crafts; and museum-related objects are specialties for sale.

Life-size model of Dinosaur *Triceratops* at Mall entrance to Museum.

The study of man and the life around him . . .

The National Museum of Natural History is one of the world's great centers for the study of man and his natural surroundings—in terms both of collections and programs of research on plants, animals, rocks, and minerals, fossil organisms, and man himself.

The millions of visitors who tour the exhibits each year usually see only a small part of the total display: The items exhibited represent only one percent of the collections totalling more than 55 million specimens of plants, animals, minerals, and artifacts that are stored in laboratories and offices elsewhere in the building where more than 100 scientists are engaged in research.

Many of these specimens date back to 19th-century expeditions which helped open up the western United States to settlement. Today they constitute an unequalled reservoir of information for researchers who need to study samples of the natural world taken before the polluting effects of modern technology became widespread. Smithsonian staff members are constantly adding new specimens taken during current expeditions to all parts of the world.

Now, to find your way around, consult the plan on p. 54 for the three floors of exhibit areas.

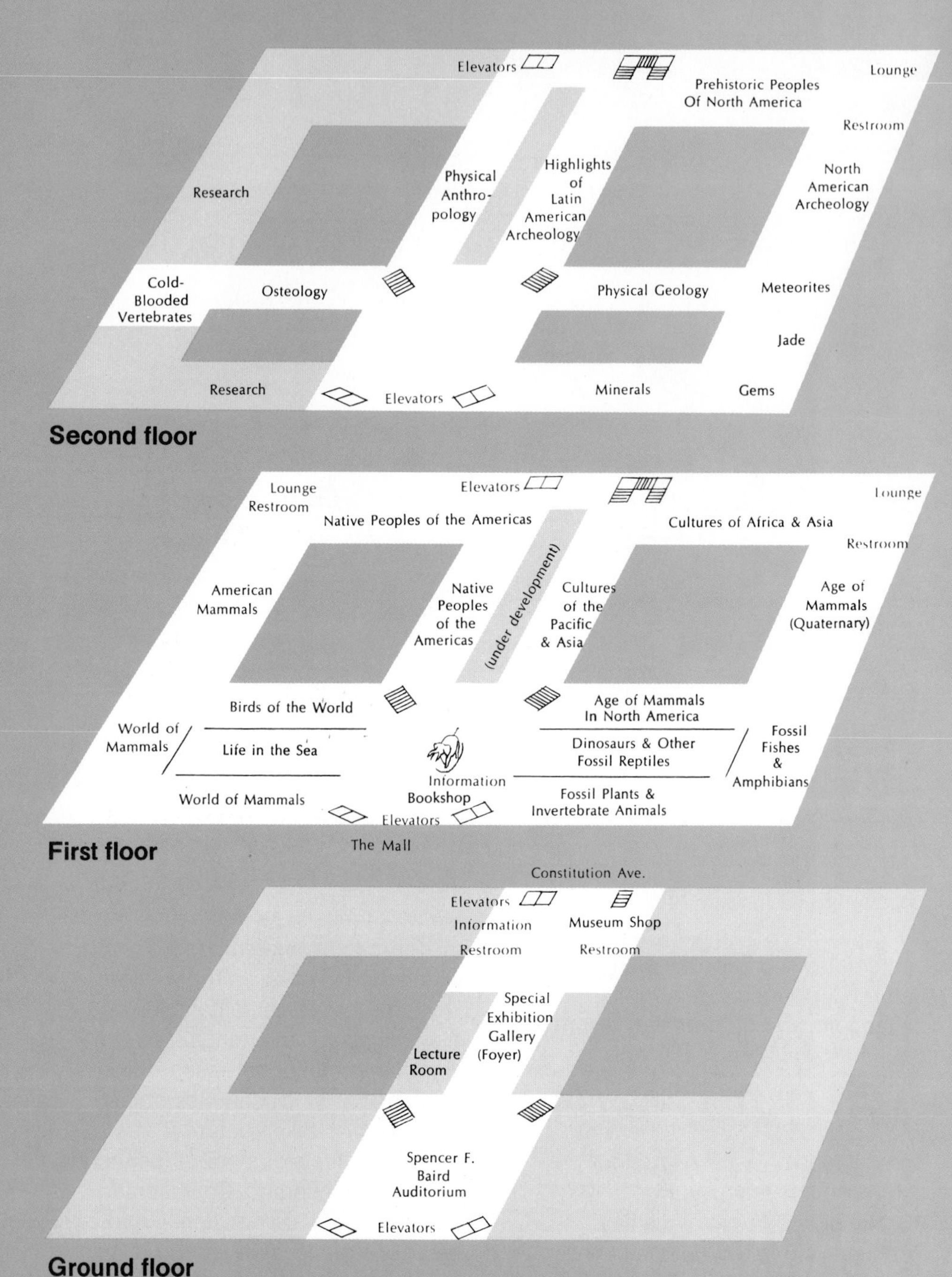

NATIONAL MUSEUM OF NATURAL HISTORY

GROUND FLOOR
Constitution Avenue Entrance – *Information*
Special Exhibits
Auditorium
Guard Office
Museum Sales Shop
Rest Rooms and Lounge

FIRST FLOOR
Mall Entrance – *Information*
Elephant *(Rotunda)*
Fossil Animals and Plants
Mammals
Life in the Sea – Blue Whale
Birds
Native Peoples of the Americas
Peoples of Africa, Asia, Pacific
Book Sales Shop
Rest Rooms and Lounge

SECOND FLOOR
Hope Diamond
Gems, Jade
Meteorites, Minerals
Our Restless Planet – *Geology*
Biology of Man – *Physical Anthropology*
North American Archeology
Prehistoric Peoples of North America
Latin American Archeology
Osteology – *Skeletons*
Amphibians and Reptiles
Rest Rooms and Lounge

GROUND FLOOR

If you enter the museum from the Constitution Avenue side you will find special exhibits straight ahead. Of particular interest, because it is believed to be the largest tiger ever taken in India, is a remarkable example of this now vanishing species. This specimen, which was 18 years old, measured eleven feet, one inch (including his tail) and weighed 857 pounds. Obtained in Uttar Pradesh, northern India, it was presented to the Smithsonian in 1969.

Also on this floor are a large auditorium and a smaller lecture room that are used for meetings, concerts, and other special events.

Stairs and elevators leading to the upper floors and the main exhibit areas of the building are located in the entrance hallway and on both sides of the auditorium.

Indian, or Bengal Tiger, believed to be the largest ever taken in India, was shot in November, 1967.

African bush elephant, the largest ever recorded.

FIRST FLOOR

Enter from the Mall and you arrive at the first-floor rotunda featuring one of the most popular exhibits—an 8-ton African bush elephant—the largest on record, and believed to be the largest that ever trod the earth, standing thirteen feet, two inches at the shoulders. Nearby, inside the entrance are huge Northwest Indian totem poles.

From the rotunda, here and on the floor above, you have access to most of the exhibit halls on each floor.

Let's go!

To make it easier to follow the route of the exhibit halls described next, we suggest you keep floor plan in hand and orient yourself to the west and east sides of the building in relation to it.

FIRST FLOOR—EAST

Fossil Plants and Invertebrate Animals

Fossil Fishes and Amphibians

Dinosaurs and Other Fossil Reptiles

These halls tell the story of how life evolved on this planet during the billions of years since it was formed. The gathering and interpreting of this evidence represents one of the great accomplishments of modern science.

The story is still incomplete, for in the more than half a billion years since the earliest known life appeared untold thousands of forms have come into being, evolved, and disappeared. Earth's seas and continents have undergone many changes—fossils of sea life may now be found in some existing land areas, hundreds of miles from the shores of present oceans and many thousands of feet above their surfaces.

The Hall of Fossil Plants and Invertebrate Animals explains the nature of fossils and the means by which their ages can be determined. Here is the oldest known fossil—the *Grinflint chert* from Northern Ontario, 1.6 billion years old. Shown in sequence are other fossil plants and animals without backbones. A series of nine dioramas shows how certain forms of life are believed to have appeared during the Paleozoic Era.

Large Trilobite fossil, Cambrian Era; from British Columbia.

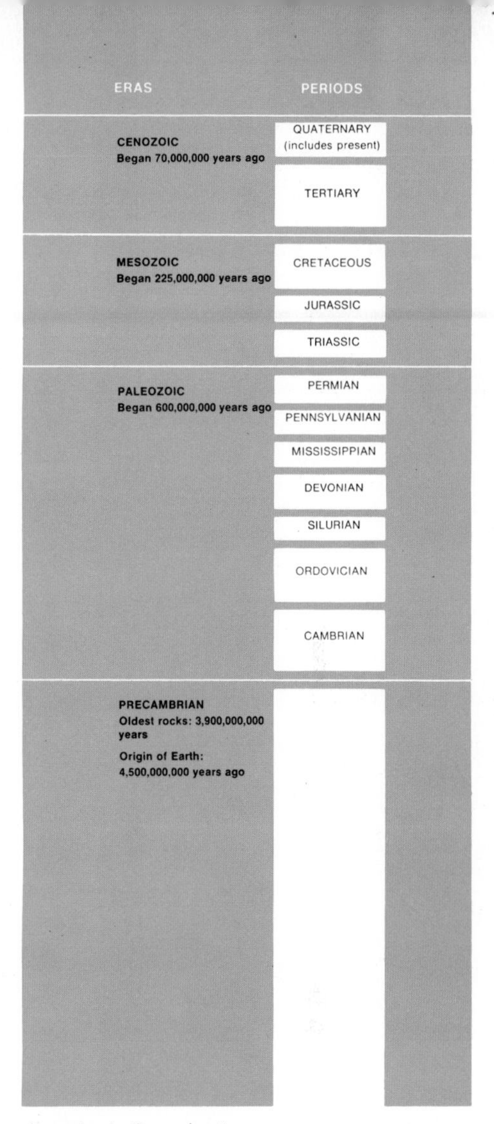

A geologic time chart.

Backboned animals are introduced in the *Hall of Fossil Fishes and Amphibians.* Displays show the development of amphibians and reptiles as life progressed from the sea onto land more than 200 million years ago during the Early Permian Period at the end of the Paleozoic Era. Among the examples shown are early jawed fishes and the first great reptiles.

One of the highlights of a Smithsonian visit is the chance to see the marvelously reconstructed skeletons of

(TOP LEFT) The Hall of Dinosaurs and other Fossil Reptiles with the *Diplodocus Longus*, one of the largest land animals.

(LEFT) Detail of a diorama depicting dinosaur life of the Mesozoic Era.

Life-size model of the *Stegosaurus Stenops* from the Late Jurassic times, about 125 million years ago.

dinosaurs dominating *The Hall of Fossil Reptiles*—and even to touch one of the bones. These enormous beasts originated, flourished, and became extinct during the Mesozoic Period. (See geologic time chart, p. 57) The great *Diplodocus*, 80 feet long, contrasts strikingly with the delicate four-foot *Camptosaurus*. Nearby are the plated *Stegosaurus* and *Triceratops;* a reconstruction of the latter stands on the Mall at the Museum entrance. Groupings of marine reptiles and vertical "slab mounts" show how other dinosaurs appeared when found in rock formation.

(ABOVE) Detail of diorama showing animals from North American plains, 20-25 million years ago.

Giant Panamanian ground sloths.

Proceed up the stairs at the east end of the hall to the balcony where colorful and dramatic scale dioramas depict dinosaurs in their own natural surroundings. High on the wall overlooking the lower level are a skeleton and a reconstruction of the awesome flying reptile, *Pterosaurus.*

The Age of Mammals

North America

The evolution of mammals in North America is traced from their expansion just after dinosaurs disappeared to the present. In this hall and adjacent areas is a series of six murals by artist Jay Matternes showing plants and animals, with mammals predominating, that flourished in the Tertiary and Quaternary Periods. Near each mural are fossil skeletons of animals living during those times—the huge 54-foot sea-dwelling *Basilosaurus;* the deer-like *Hypertragulus;* and skulls of marine mammals from nearby Calvert Cliffs, along Chesapeake Bay. A scale diorama shows a shovel-tusked mastodon, a large camel, a short-legged rhinoceros, and other extinct species.

Quaternary Age

The Quaternary Age Hall shows mammals of the latest Ice Age, which ended some 10,000 years ago on this continent. Included are reconstructed skeletons of giant ground sloths from Panama, the American mastodon and woolly mammoth. A nearby display shows how prehistoric animals were trapped in the La Brea tar pits of California.

Diorama of male initiation rites, Luvale people of Zambia and Angola.

Buddhist art in Korea, Koryo Dynasty, A.D. 918-1392.

Still at the East of the building—in the center and on the north, or Constitution Avenue, side—are Halls of the

Cultures of Africa and Asia

Cultures of the Pacific and Asia

The diversity of the cultures of Africa and Asia is dramatically displayed in a series of exhibits dealing with many facets of the heritage and the daily life of the peoples dwelling in these areas.

Africa

Step inside a reproduced Herero hut from south-central Africa; and listen to the drums reverberating around the entrance. This is but one of many displays illustrating the background of the peoples of Africa south of the Sahara, from which much of today's American Black culture is derived. Aspects of hunting and farming; religion, arts and music; crafts and textiles; metalwork are featured throughout the exhibit area in relation to many African tribes—the Bushmen, Hottentot, Himba, Somali, Amhara, the warring tribes of Rwanda, and the culture of ancient Zimbabwe in what is now Rhodesia. There are some splendid examples of Benin brasswork from West Africa dating to the 13th century, and other masks and figures of the type attracting so much artistic interest today.

One of the most popular showcases is that of the Music of Africa showing drums, zithers, flutes, and other tonal instruments that are used for both music and for signals. Push a button and hear the tribal rhythms of these instruments come to life and, as you listen to the variety of instruments which are shaken or thumped to accompany dances, watch slide projections of instruments being played.

Similar treatment of the backgrounds of peoples from northern Africa and the Middle East is highlighted in displays of their crafts, objects of

A Chinese opera. Scene from *The Second Return to the Palace.*

Yap stone money.

Bali, Monkey King of Kish Kindhya in a sacred dance drama of India.

daily life, and the religions of Islam and Judaism.

The Pacific and Asia

The various nationalities of Asia and the Far East are covered in a variety of exhibit forms. A charming central display shows everyday objects in the form of Japanese Folk Crafts. A model of a Shinto shrine tells something of the leading Japanese religion, while Confucianism and Buddhism are represented by artifacts and explanations. Reproduction of a room from a Korean house, objects from the Ryukyus, Tibet, and China treat everyday life, as well as music, language, and the accouterments of Oriental calligraphy.

In this area surely the liveliest—and loudest—exhibit is that depicting a scene from a Chinese opera. This art form, which has been much publicized in recent years, dates back to the late 13th century under the Yuan Dynasty. By pushing a button you may study

Cats of the world.

Bighorn sheep.

the figures involved in the opera, *The Second Return to the Palace,* while you listen to the eerie (to Western ears), cacophonous sounds that accompany this striking traditional entertainment of China.

The area of the world so long in the headlines, Southern Asia, is brought to the West through displays of the music and crafts of Thailand, India, and Pakistan. The ancient Khmer culture of Cambodia is represented by objects of daily life; one exhibit case is filled with the delightful shadow puppets of Malaysia.

Other displays of Pacific Cultures feature bark painting by aborigines from Arnhem Land; descriptions of sailing and fishing in Polynesia; rice growing in the Philippines; stone money from Yap in the Caroline Islands; and one of the remarkable and mysterious stone figures from the Easter Islands.

FIRST FLOOR—WEST

The World of Mammals

These halls display hundreds of animals in life-like settings. Near the entrance a large mural shows the origins of mammals around the world, color-keyed to locations on the map. Exhibits explain classifications of animals, their environment, and aspects of their relationship to man.

Animals displayed range from gorillas, orangutans, and monkeys to lions with their cubs, zebras, antelopes, and giraffes. The subtle colorings of these galleries, with earth tones predominating, accentuate the natural habitat settings in which the animals are shown.

American Mammals

North American mammals occupy the west side of the building. Twelve large exhibits show, in true-to-life backgrounds, groups of caribou, wolves, bison, moose, deer, and bears—all native to this continent.

Life in the Sea

In this dramatically lit hall hangs what is surely the largest single exhibit in the museum—a life-size (92-feet long), Fiberglas model of a blue whale—the largest animal that ever lived. Behind it other whales are shown in outline illustrating their sizes and shapes, and around it are models of sharks, sailfish, and porpoises. Against varying shades of blue-green walls, evocative of the sea, exhibits show different types of sea life through film projections and preserved specimens—fish, crustaceans, corals, mollusks, sponges. The process of "freeze-drying"—the most advanced method of preserving animal specimens—is explained with examples of the process.

Blue whale, *Sibbaldus musculus.*

(RIGHT) Martha, last of the passenger pigeons, died in 1914.

(BELOW RIGHT) Bird's eggs of different species.

Birds of the World

Specimens from the world's major land and ocean areas are displayed in realistic settings, accentuating differences in form, size, and coloration. Exhibits illustrate migration, reproduction, feeding habits, flight, and ways in which birds have been important to man.

Colorful groupings show birds of special interest, such as the ostrich, complete with babies just out of their eggs; the argus pheasant noted for its enormous plumes; the now extinct passenger pigeon and Carolina parakeet; and the universally appealing Antarctic penguins. Overhead are life-size paintings of various birds in flight.

Native Peoples of the Americas

The New World peoples showed a high degree of imagination and skill in using the resources of their environment. Realistic scenes show the appearance and traditional ways of life of those who held the continents from Point Barrow in the Arctic to Tierra del Fuego and Cape Horn in the south before European discovery.

Eskimo life is displayed with clothing, hunting and fishing equipment, styles of homelife, ivory carving, and other native arts. In one life-size exhibit Polar Eskimos with their sled dogs gather around laughing at a young boy who has just caught an undersized seal through the ice.

The Indians of North America are featured in many exhibits explaining their individual specialties and modes of living. On display are a birch-bark canoe of the Woodland Indian; the great wampum belt of Union representing the Tecumseh Confederation of 1800; a Plains Indian tipi made of fourteen buffalo cowskins; Sitting Bull's Winchester rifle; bonnets and crowns of feathers; items from a potlatch feast of the Kwakiuti Indians; totem poles; and many other objects.

Near the elevator, in the north corridor, a map mural shows the

(RIGHT) Totem from northwest Haida Indians.

(LEFT) Clothing of late 19th-century Apache Indians.

(BELOW) Polar Eskimo diorama.

resourcefulness of the natives of North and South America in utilizing the local gifts of nature.

Indians of the Western United States, Mexico, Central and South America are represented by many displays showing their unique methods of going about their daily lives. Maps in the exhibit area locate the origins of the tribes in relation to today's geographic boundaries. A model of a Pueblo village; Navaho crafts and silverwork; Hopi snake dancers; items belonging to the Hupa, Apache, Pima, and Mohave all comprise a sweeping look at characteristic tribal customs.

The story continues with exhibits of the descendants of the Mayas in Guatemala; the Aymara of the Andes; the shrunken heads of the Jivaro of Ecuador; Carib and Arawak tribes of the Guianan rain forests; Argentine's Tehuelche (bola-using horsemen); and the Yahgan and Ona from Tierra Del Fuego.

A diorama shows Lucayan Indians coming upon Columbus when he landed in the Bahamas on October 16, 1492. Nearby are relics of the first Indians who met Columbus.

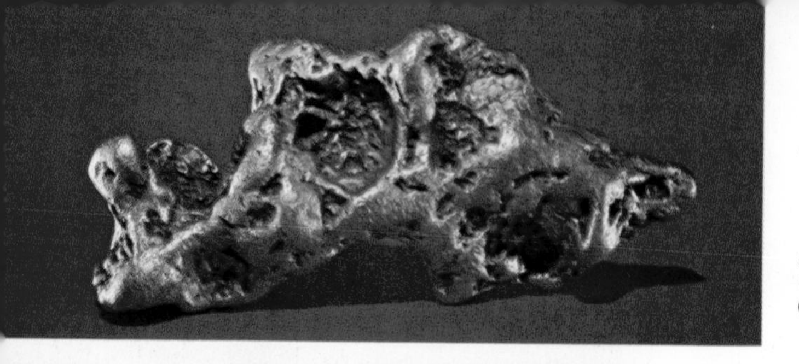

(LEFT) Nugget of California gold weighing 82 ounces.

(CENTER LEFT) Calcite (calcium carbonate) crystals from Cumberland, England.

(BOTTOM LEFT) Although looking like a plant fossil, the lacy mineral specimen is a *dendrite pyrolusite* crystal formed along a bedding plane of shale.

SECOND FLOOR—EAST

From the rotunda, exhibits on the east side of the building may be seen in this order . . .

Minerals, Gems, Jade, Meteorites

Welcome to the *Mineral Kingdom.*

These Halls of Mineral Sciences contain one of the world's finest collections of gems and minerals, and the settings add to the breathtaking qualities of the specimens.

The properties of various minerals are shown by means of hundreds of samples selected from the Smithsonian's extensive research collection. Introductory exhibits in the hall define the various species, show how they are formed and found, and illustrate such special qualities as the almost incredible property of fluorescence under ultraviolet light.

Huge gypsum crystals from the Mexican Cave of Swords; a startling example of amethyst crystals from Brazil; a sliced and polished jade boulder from China are but some of the beautiful and rare items displayed in the light and airy halls. Many

(*RIGHT*) Section of Gem Room showing crystal ball.

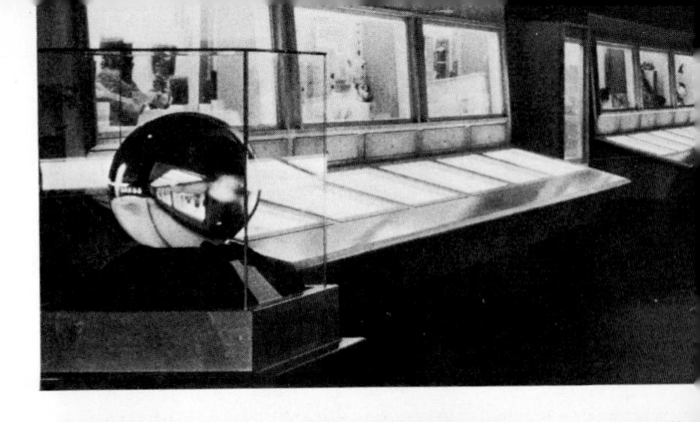

outstanding specimens are from the Frederick A. Canfield and Washington A. Roebling collections.

Gems

Now, for a real Smithsonian highlight! Beginning with the gold carpeting, you know you are in a very special kind of museum display area when you enter the *Hall of Gems.* The first question from everyone who enters is, "Where is it?" And *IT,* the Hope Diamond, is directly ahead, secured in its glass-faced vault, resting on white brocade, finding the culmination of its legendary history in the admiring stares of its viewers.

Probably the world's most famous diamond, it may not be as big as you had imagined, but it is very, very blue. By speculation, it is linked to the famous "French Blue," which was brought to France from India in 1668 to become part of the crown jewels of Louis XIV. The French Blue was stolen in 1792 and never recovered, but in 1830 an extraordinary 44.5-carat blue diamond—presumably cut from the missing gem—came on the market. It was purchased by Henry Thomas Hope of England, thus acquiring its present name. In 1949 the gem was acquired from the estate of Mrs. Evalyn Walsh McLean by the New York jewelry firm of Harry Winston, Inc. who, ten years later, presented it to the Smithsonian in Mrs. McLean's original setting.

While the Hope may be the best known, there are other remarkable diamonds and other gems of unique sizes and colors—the 127-carat

The Hope Diamond.

Portuguese diamond; the Eugenie Blue diamond, 31 carats and heart-shaped. The Logan sapphire is 423 carats, and The Star of Asia, weighing 330 carats, is one of the finest star sapphires in the world with a strong, sharply defined, 6-rayed star. Hundreds of exquisite cut stones shine through the exhibit cases and the wall cabinets which show them off to superb advantage.

(RIGHT) Tucson Meteorite in Meteorite Hall.

(BELOW) Chinese carved jade covered vessel.

Jade

A small but elegant hall adjacent to the gems contains part of the Smithsonian's assemblage of jade in beautiful colors and forms. Largely the gift of the Maude Monell Vetlesen estate, there are screens, vessels, bowls, incense burners, scepters, and candlesticks produced mostly during the Ching Dynasty (1644-1912) when the art of jade carving was at its peak.

Meteorites

Looking like a piece of contemporary sculpture, the *Tucson Meteorite* found in Arizona in the middle of the last century is but one example of these specimens from outer space that have plummeted to earth. The hall exhibits and describes various kinds of meteorites, showing where they have been found and the effects of their impacts. A wall map with tiny lights shows locations of meteorite falls and finds in the United States.

Overhead, at the end of the hall, a moon model shows the landing sites of the Apollo Flights.

Physical Geology

Our Restless Planet is introduced with a remarkable Earth Globe showing in different colors such geologic features as ancient crust, volcanic rocks, plains, mountain belts, islands, oceanic ridges, and the floor of the sea. To the left is a dramatic mural of Earth's place in the solar system. Rocks of various kinds and ores such as iron, copper, and silver are exhibited with explanations of how they are formed and where they occur. Of interest is the Ontonagon copper boulder, an object of Indian veneration prior to its discovery by an adventurous Englishman near Lake Superior in 1766.

Between this Hall and the Halls of Mineral Sciences a picture window provides a great view of the dinosaurs on the floor below.

A Geologist's View of the Earth.

The Ontonagon copper boulder.

Wood carving from
Spiro Mound, Oklahoma.

Diorama showing inhabitants of the area now Washington, D.C. as they appeared five hundred years ago.

Diorama of Soapstone Quarry, Santa Catalina Island, California.

Prehistoric Peoples of North America

North American Archeology

The period beginning with the first evidence of man on this continent, between 25,000 and 40,000 years ago, to his final subjugation by European and other American invaders in the 19th century is covered in these two halls.

The diverse character of the ancient cultures reflects differing adjustments to widely varying environments—from the Arctic and western America to the deserts of the Southwest, from the grasslands of the Great Plains to the eastern woodlands and the Florida Everglades.

Lively wall displays show how "Modern Science Dates the Past" through carbon-14, tree ring, and pollen methods available to today's archeologist.

Ceremonial specimens from an Oklahoma burial ground; textiles; native pottery, and prehistoric sculptures are rare examples of ancient life. A life-size scene shows Indians

(RIGHT) Chac Mool, Toltec Maya site of Chichen Itza, Yucatan, 987-1204 A.D.

(BELOW LEFT) Replica of the golden *Crocodile God,* Sitio Conte site in Cocle Province, Panama, 800-1400 A.D.

Cast of Olmec culture stone head, discovered and excavated by a Smithsonian scientist in southern Mexico, 1946.

of the Potomac Valley, another deals with the Indians of Pueblo Bonito in what is now New Mexico.

The spread of tobacco, stone-shaping arts, aboriginal mines and quarries, and the exchange of European metal and glass trade goods are other features.

Latin American Archeology

The history of the Indians of Mexico, Central America, the Antilles, and South America is summarized from their origins more than 10,000 years ago to the time of the Spanish conquest in the 16th century. Exhibit groupings correspond to the various prehistoric culture areas of those regions—Marginal, Tropical Forest, Circum-Caribbean, Meso-American, and Andean. Carefully selected specimens of the Aztec, Maya, and Inca civilizations are supplemented by maps, models, and photographs illustrating their achievements in architecture, sculpture, pottery, textiles, and other fields of endeavor.

SECOND FLOOR—WEST

Physical Anthropology

Beginning with *Man's Primate Heritage* these exhibits deal with man in terms of his biology and evolution. Modern man is distinguished from other primates by notable characteristics—among them upright posture, digital dexterity, verbal ability. The *Biology of Human Population* shows how racial growth (in height) and development (in proportions) are influenced by environmental factors, nutrition, and health. Mummification, surgical alterations of the body, and other human alterations, such as tattooing, are treated in the section, *Modification of the Human Body.* A stunning life-size mural shows examples of bound feet, pierced lower lips, tooth alteration, and so on. *Varieties of Modern Man* displays racial differences; and a large wall map with models of mounted heads in various locations gives details on, and differences in, physical characteristics showing that *Modern Man Has Many Forms.* A bust shows how Zinjanthropus, a man-like creature who lived two million years ago, may have looked.

Osteology

Skeletons of various mammals, birds, reptiles, amphibians, and fishes are posed characteristically and grouped by orders to illustrate their relationships. Skeletons of man and the great apes standing together demonstrate their affinity in the Order of Primates. Bone structures of a variety of animals are compared to show their evolution and adaptation to environment.

Cold-Blooded Vertebrates

Habitat groups illustrate the mode of life of reptiles and amphibians in the desert and the Florida Everglades. Other aspects highlight their feeding habits, methods of locomotion, and economic influence on man.

History and growth of the collections

At the time the Smithsonian was founded in 1846, the Act of Establishment specified that "all objects of natural history, plants, and geological and mineral specimens belonging to the United States" be deposited with it. Not until 1857, however, did Congress appropriate funds to maintain such a museum and it was

(LEFT PAGE) Diorama showing various physical forms of modern man.

(RIGHT) Comparison of skeletons of man and manlike apes.

at that time, under Smithsonian management, that a start was made toward gathering all such collections under one roof.

In the middle of the last century, primarily under the auspices of the distinguished naturalist, Spencer Fullerton Baird, the Smithsonian began to develop as a repository for collections. Baird's objective was to record and preserve for future scientists the natural history of this new land before it became obscured or forever lost under the inexorable march of "progress." Thanks to his efforts and those of the dedicated professionals and amateurs who collaborated in the projects, the museum soon became preeminent.

Within a short time the collections outgrew the space available for them within the Smithsonian building, and early in this century Congress gave the go-ahead for a separate building for the museum.

Building

Authorized by Congress in 1903, the original, central portion of this granite-faced building was designed in classical style by Washington architects Hornblower & Marshall. Completed in 1911, the building was first used in 1908, and some exhibits were opened to the public in March 1910.

The original part of the building, measuring 561 by 365 feet, has an octagonal rotunda 80 feet across and 125 feet high, and contains almost ten acres of space on five floors. The two upper floors contain curators' offices, laboratories, and storage areas. The first and second floors contain the main exhibit halls, and the ground floor (Constitution Avenue) contains space for short-term exhibitions, the Auditorium, service facilities, and the main Smithsonian library.

Construction of east and west wings was authorized in 1930, but funds for them were not provided until 1958. Designed by Washington architects Mills, Petticord & Mills, both were completed and occupied by 1965. They measure 199 by 180 feet and bring the total length of the building to 897 feet, doubling its floor area.

Model monoplane 1911

Rocket row along the western side of the Arts and Industries Building.

National Air and Space Museum

MICHAEL COLLINS, Director

Arts and Industries Building
Mall: South side at 9th St., S.W.

Air and Space Building
(Temporary building)
Independence Avenue and 9th St., S.W.
Open: Both buildings open daily except Christmas
Hours: 10:00 a.m. to 5:30 p.m. (later in summer)
Telephone: (202) 628-4422

NOTE: We suggest that visitors to the National Air and Space Museum first see the collection in the Arts and Industries Building (Wright Brothers' airplane; *Spirit of St. Louis;* *Apollo 11* command module; moon landing module; moon rock) and then proceed to the nearby Air and Space Building.

Display illustrating the principle of hot-air ascension.

What's going on and where to find it

Information Desk
Located near the entrance of the Arts and Industries Building, with up-to-date information on special exhibits, lectures, and other activities. Phone: 381-6264.

Guided Tours
For school groups. Must be scheduled four weeks in advance. Phone: 381-6471.

Museum Shop
Near the entrance of the Arts and Industries Building. Books, post cards, slides, posters, models, and souvenirs, especially relating to man's conquest of air and space, are for sale.

Airplanes from the World War I Aircraft exhibit.

The National Air and Space Museum

Man's dream to fly is as old as man himself, and deeply imbedded in his myths and tales. But the practical realization of this dream had to wait until late in the 18th century when, for the first time, man ascended above earth in balloons. From that time to the air age—and, in recent decades, to the conquest of space—stretches an inspiring story of man's ingenuity, heroism, and achievement. So much of this took place in the United States that many of the most significant accomplishments of flight are represented by actual objects collected in this country during the last two generations.

The Collections

The Museum has more than 240 historic or technologically significant aircraft, 40 spacecraft, 50 missiles and rockets, 425 aero engines, 350 propellers, hundreds of scale models, aviation uniforms, awards, instruments, flight equipment, and many unique items of memorabilia pertaining to famous inventors, airmen, and events. Only a small portion of the collection can be on display at any one time. A significant number are on loan to other museums throughout the world.

Model of building being erected for The National Air and Space Museum.

The *Kitty Hawk Flyer*. (BELOW) The *Spirit of St. Louis*.

New Building Planned

Now under construction at Congressional authorization is a major new building which will carry out the Museum's objective of providing a national center for exhibition, study, and public education in the broad field of air and space. The building is being constructed on the south side of the Mall between Fourth and Seventh Streets. Designed by the St. Louis architect, Gyo Obata, it is scheduled to open during 1976—the Bicentennial Year. In addition to a greatly increased exhibit area and major innovative exhibits, it will also include larger library and research facilities. Improved study facilities for staff and visiting scholars will make it one of the world's great centers of aerospace research.

Apollo 11 command module, *Columbia*.

Arts and Industries Building

Because of limited space, exhibits are changed periodically. Schedules at the entrance will tell you what special exhibits are on view and where the best known objects are on display.

Enter the building from the Mall and you are in the vaulted North Hall. On some 1,700 square feet of floor space and in the air space above are displayed original engines of flight that indelibly marked the history of the 20th century.

Above you hangs suspended the Wright Brothers' *Kitty Hawk Flyer.* It is now almost impossible to conceive that cold morning of December 17, 1903, when Orville and Wilbur Wright became the first men to fly successfully a powered and controlled heavier-than-air plane. On the first flight of the day, Orville Wright, handling the controls as he lay prone on the wing, succeeded in flying the *Kitty Hawk* some 500 feet across the sandy slopes of Kill Devil Hill at Kitty Hawk, North Carolina. The air age had begun.

Behind the *Kitty Hawk,* as if following in its wake, hangs another epoch-making plane—Charles Lindbergh's *Spirit of St. Louis.* This is the aircraft which Lindbergh piloted across the Atlantic on the first solo, transatlantic non-stop flight. Leaving New York on May 20, 1927, he landed in triumph in Paris 33 hours and 28 minutes later.

Nearby is the original command module, *Columbia,* of the Apollo 11 mission (July 16-24, 1969). Behind it is an authentic Lunar Landing Module (LM-2), identical to the one that carried astronauts Neil Armstrong and Edwin Aldrin to the surface of the moon.

"... one small step for a man, one giant leap for mankind."
Astronaut Neil Armstrong as he set foot on the lunar surface on July 20, 1969

Other space capsules on exhibit are:
Freedom 7 First United States manned space flight 1961
Friendship 7 First United States manned orbiting flight 1962
Gemini IV First United States space walk 1965

Other space-related items shown are astronauts' space suits, life-support systems, food, and hygienic, as well as photographic, equipment.

Early Smithsonian activity in the development of flight is represented by the engine used in Secretary Samuel P. Langley's flight experiments of 1903, together with a model of the "Aerodrome" it powered.

Another display shows some experimental rockets developed by Dr. Robert H. Goddard, the "father of liquid-fueled rocketry," who on March 16, 1926, launched successfully his first test model.

Here, too, in a dramatic mounting is a "gem" from the lunar surface, a one-pound (478.8 grams) rock brought back by the Apollo 11 astronauts from the first moon landing.

Elsewhere in Arts and Industries . . .

In nearby halls are other historic aircraft, gliders, engines, and models, as well as temporary exhibits of various kinds dealing with aerospace history and development.

Displayed are a number of small-plane engines, including the Curtiss OX-5

Friendship 7 capsule.

Apollo Lunar Landing Module (LM-2).

(1914-18) that powered the Curtiss Jenny; a Pratt & Whitney Wasp, Jr. (1940)—a type still in use today. Among those in the aeropropulsion section, in addition to a representative sample of model-plane engines, are a supercharged Liberty of 1922; a Packard (Rolls-Royce) Merlin of 1944, and a Wright Turbo Cyclone of 1954. Jet engines include a Whittle W1-X of 1941; a General Electric Turbojet of 1944; and a prototype of the Pratt & Whitney J-57 of 1949, the type used to power the Boeing 707. Nearby stands a *Hawker Hurricane II* of Battle of Britain fame, together with an example of the Rolls-Royce Merlin engine that powered both it and the *Supermarine Spitfire.* A display memorializes the American Eagle Squadron, which flew the *Hurricane* in that historic battle.

As you leave the Arts and Industries Building, turn to the left and walk the few yards along *Rocket Row.* Here you see a *Jupiter C*, launch vehicle for the first United States satellite, *Explorer I*; a Vanguard rocket which launched the second United States satellite; the submarine-launched *Polaris* missile; and an *Atlas D* intercontinental ballistic missile. Now you are at the . . .

Air and Space Building

This temporary building contains a series of dioramas, photographs, and models which trace the history of flight from the days of balloons and kites to the present. Among actual planes exhibited in this building is the *Vin Fiz*, the first airplane to fly coast-to-coast in 1911. Built by the Wright brothers, it took off from Sheepshead

Lunar rock collected by Apollo 11 astronauts.

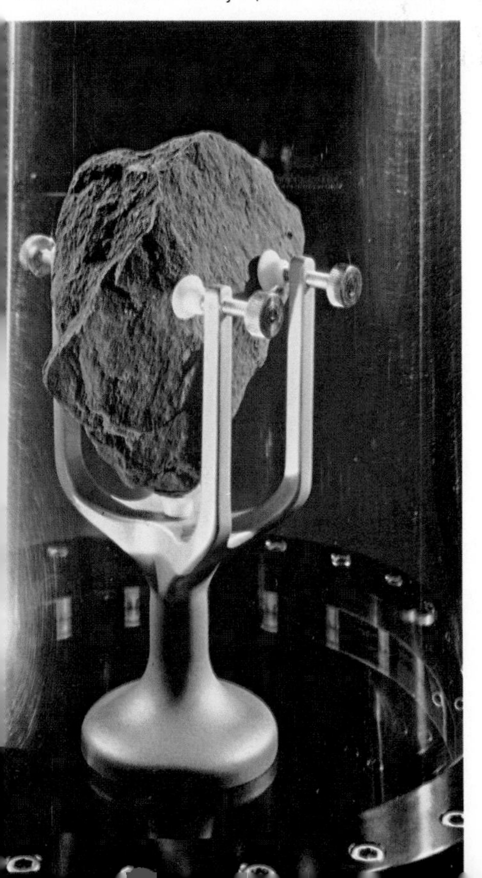

The *Atlas-D* rocket—the first U.S. Air Force intercontinental ballistic missile (ICBM).

Bell X-1. First aircraft to fly faster than sound in level flight.

Bay, New York, on September 17, 1911, and arrived in Long Beach, California 84 days and 70 landings later. Average speed: 52 m.p.h.

Behind it stands the Lockheed 5-C Vega, *Winnie Mae*, the first airplane to fly twice around the world. Both times Wiley Post was at the controls, flying solo during the second trip, July 15-22, 1933.

Winnie Mae, flown by Wiley Post during his 1931 and 1933 around-the-world flights.

Elsewhere is the Bell X-1 named *Glamorous Glennis* in which Captain Charles F. Yeager first broke the sound barrier in level flight on October 14, 1947. Space-related items are a *Discoverer XIII*, the world's first space vehicle recovered after carrying an instrument package on 17 polar orbits (1960); *Tiros* (1960) and *Nimbus* (1966) weather satellites; as well as *Early Bird* and *Intelsat* communications satellites (1965). Also shown is the RVX 1-5 nose cone, the first re-entry nose cone to be recovered after a space flight of intercontinental range—more than 6,325 statute miles.

An important milestone on the way to the moon is NASA's unmanned *Surveyor* spacecraft that soft-landed on the lunar surface where it took the thousands of photos and data required to design Project Apollo's lunar module—the space vehicle that enabled the United States to land the first man on the moon.

A Gemini flight simulator permits young visitor participation in space rendezvous and docking maneuvers.

The *Experimentarium* (for Experi-

Vin Fiz (Wright EX). First airplane to fly coast-to-coast.

mental Air and Space Planetarium) stands near the center of the building. Designed to enable viewers to visualize and understand space flight and the wonders of outer space, its presentation techniques are forerunners of what will be seen in the projected *Spacearium* at the future building of the National Air and Space Museum. From time to time the Experimentarium will offer innovative presentations to measure audience reactions to new program techniques.

History

Shortly after its establishment, the Smithsonian became involved with the progress of flight. Its first Secretary, Joseph Henry, recommended to President Lincoln that balloons be used for aerial reconnaissance. In June 1861 the Institution sponsored a successful demonstration of balloons on the Mall that contributed to their use in the Civil War. Samuel P. Langley, the third Secretary, designed and constructed a number of unmanned heavier-than-air craft between 1887 and 1903, of which two successfully flew under steam power for more than half a mile. In 1915 Secretary Charles Walcott was instrumental in founding the National Advisory Committee for Aeronautics, which later evolved into the National Aeronautics and Space Administration. He also arranged Smithsonian financial support for early experiments in rocket propulsion by Robert H. Goddard.

The National Air and Space Museum, which originated as the Section of Aeronautics in the United States National Museum, was established by Congress in August 1946 as a separate National Air Museum. In 1966 this name was expanded to accord recognition to the nation's space-flight activities, and in 1967 the Museum was officially made responsible for preserving and displaying space craft and related materials produced by the National Aeronautics and Space Administration.

Building

The original Department of Arts and Industries was organized to house the gift of exhibits from the Philadelphia Centennial Exposition of 1876. Congress appropriated funds in 1879 to construct a National Museum building next to the "Castle," and in this polychrome brick companion to the original Smithsonian building the collections were first exhibited in the 1880s. The growing aeronautical collections were included in this departmental concept and remained in the building after removal of the history and technology collections to their own museum in 1964.

Detail, *Peacock Room*

(*RIGHT*) Persian metalwork, 6-5th century B.C. Achaemenid.

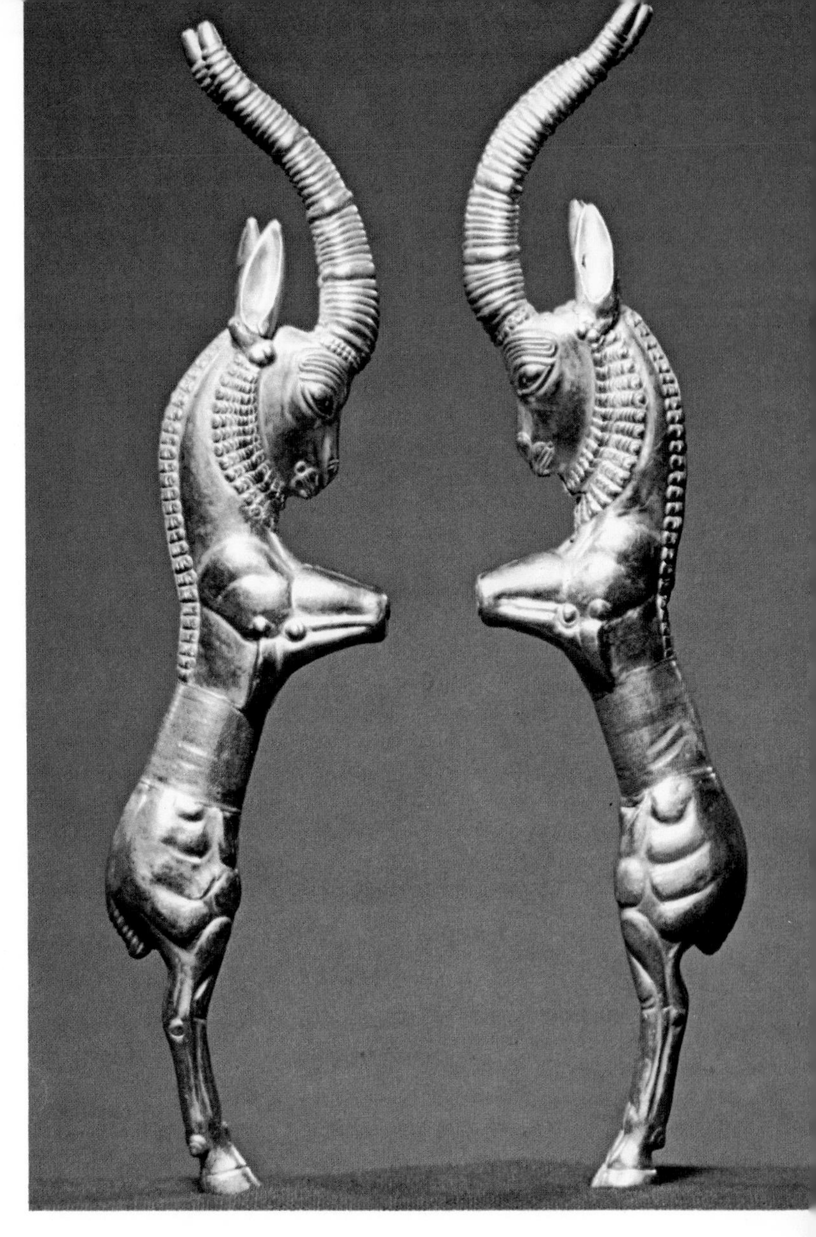

Freer Gallery of Art

HAROLD P. STERN, Director

Mall: South side at 12th St., S.W.
Open: Daily except Christmas
Hours: 10:00 a.m. to 5:30 p.m.
Telephone: (202) 381-5344

What's going on and where to find it

Information Desk
Located inside the main entrance, with up-to-date information on special exhibitions, tours, and other current activities. Telephone: (202) 381-6264.

Guided Tours
Arrangements for school or adult groups must be made two weeks in advance. Telephone: (202) 381-5344.

Sales Desk
Located inside the main entrance. For sale are Freer publications describing and illustrating the collections, prints and postcards, reproductions of selected items from the collections.

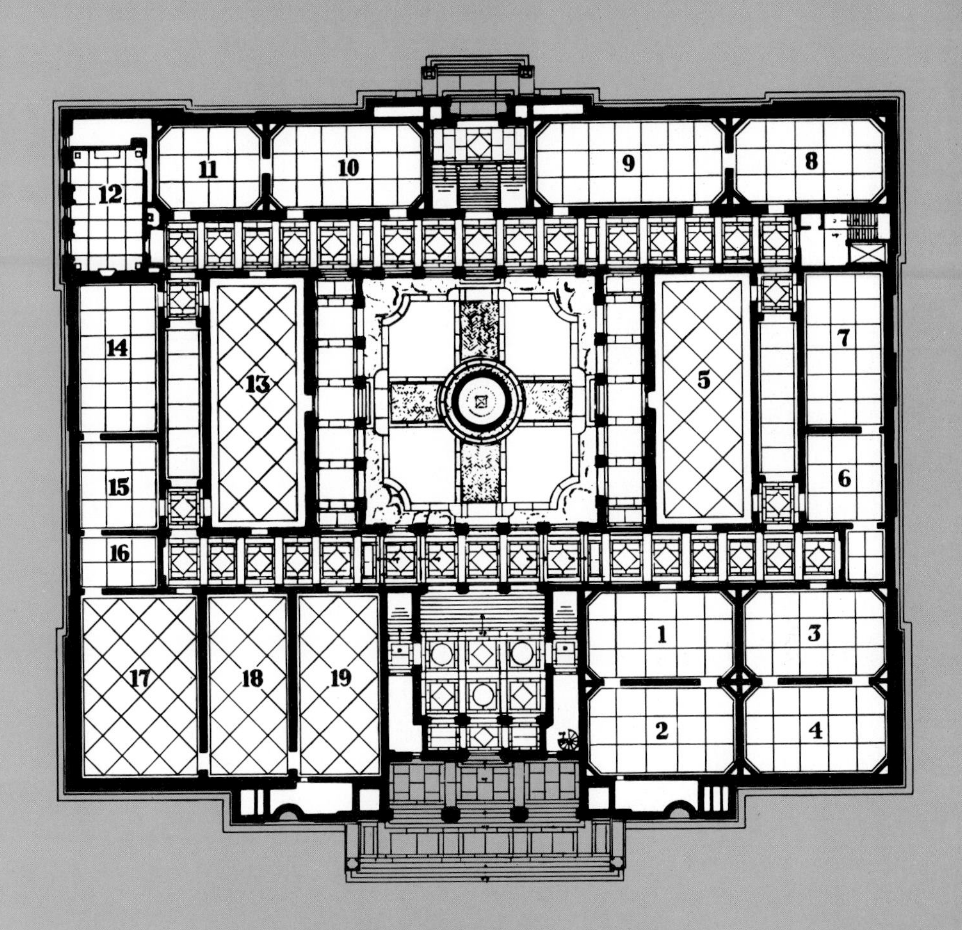

THE FREER GALLERY OF ART

The Freer Gallery of Art presents one of the Western Hemisphere's more distinguished collections of art from the Far East and the Near East. It also contains an important collection of works by American artists, of whom many were friends or contemporaries of the founder, Charles Lang Freer.

1-5 *Japanese*
West corridor—*Korean*
6-7 *Near Eastern, Islamic*
8 *Indian*
9 *American painters*
10-11 *Changing Exhibitions*
12 *Whistler's Peacock Room*
East corridor—*Chinese*
13-19 *Chinese*

Exhibits in galleries 12 and 17 are permanent, but those in the others are subject to periodic change, since only a fraction of the Freer's more than 10,000 catalogued works of art can be displayed at one time.

Collections

Art of the Far East, Mid-Orient, and Near East

China
Bronzes, paintings, sculpture in stone and bronze, pottery and porcelain, jade, lacquer.

Japan
Paintings, sculpture in wood, bronze and lacquer, pottery and porcelain, works in metal and lacquer.

Korea
Paintings, pottery, bronzes.

India
Paintings, sculpture, pottery, metalwork, manuscripts.

Iran
Paintings, sculpture, pottery, metalwork, manuscripts.

Egypt and Syria
Sculpture, glass, pottery, manuscripts.

Also in the collections are Greek, Aramaic, and Armenian biblical manuscripts; and, from the Early Christian period, paintings, gold, and silver.

(ABOVE) Ukiyo-e-style painting by Utagawa Toyoharu, 1735-1814.

(RIGHT) Bronze tiger, Chou dynasty, 9th century B.C.

White earthenware jar. Shang dynasty, 12-11th century, B.C.

American Art

Foremost among the American artists represented in the Freer collections is James Abbott McNeill Whistler, upon whose advice Charles Freer originally turned his attention to Oriental art. The Freer has the largest assemblage in any one place of the paintings, drawings, and prints of Whistler. His *Peacock Room*, executed in 1877 for a British merchant, is one of the Gallery's most striking displays.

Other American works include paintings by Brush, Dewing, Hassam, Homer, Melchers, Metcalf, Murphy, Platt, Ryder, Sargent, Smith, Thayer, Tryon, and Twachtman; and sculptures by Saint-Gaudens.

View of the *Peacock Room*.

Peacock Room with painting, *Fox and Silver: The Princess from the Land of Porcelain,* James McNeill Whistler.

History

When Detroit industrialist Charles Lang Freer deeded his art collection to the Nation in 1906, President Theodore Roosevelt hailed the gift as

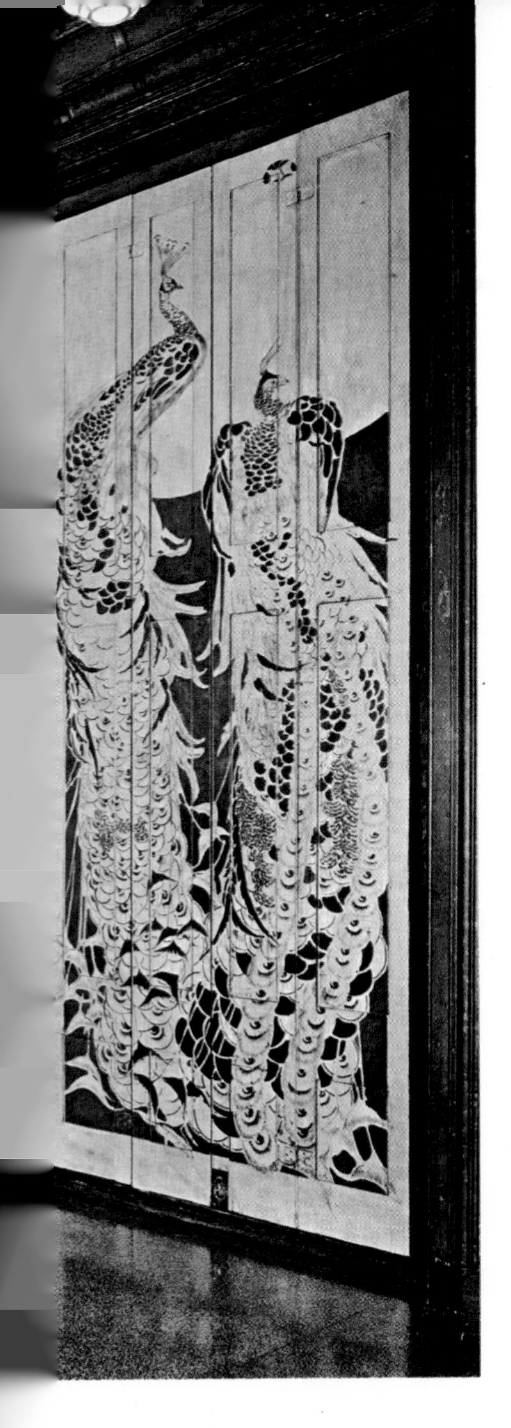

ɔne of the most valuable collections
hich any private individual has
ver given to any people."

he deed of gift included both funds
ɔ construct a museum and an endowment for the study and care of the collection. His will stipulated that no further additions be made to the American collection after his death (he died in 1919), and specifically forbade loans from, or to, the collection. It directed that the endowment income be used to add to the Oriental collection suitable objects of the highest quality and, at the same time, to carry on research in the civilizations of the countries of Asia in which the objects were produced.

As a result, through the years the Freer collection has been continuously and importantly augmented, so that today the Gallery is regarded as a leading center of research in the various fields of Oriental art. In close collaboration with the University of Michigan, it trains graduate students majoring in Oriental art, and from universities and museums in all parts of the world scholars regularly come to study and work in its collections.

Freer publications, by members of its staff and other leading scholars, are to be found in libraries and museums all over the world.

Building

The Freer Gallery was designed by Charles A. Platt in the style of a Florentine Renaissance palace. It was built of pink granite quarried near Milford, Massachusetts, and measures approximately 228 by 185 by 46 feet high. The exhibition galleries, all on the upper floor, surround an open garden court 65 feet square, with the offices, laboratories, library, and workrooms all on the lower, ground floor. The building was formally opened to the public in May 1923.

Joseph H. Hirshhorn Museum and Sculpture Garden

Model of the building.

ABRAM LERNER, Director

The Mall: South side at 8th Street, S.W.
Telephone: (202) 628-4422

Opening scheduled for Fall 1974

Just east of the Arts and Industries Building, the Hirshhorn Museum and Sculpture Garden will be the permanent home of the magnificent collection of painting and sculpture donated to the United States in 1966 by American financier Joseph H. Hirshhorn.

Called by Secretary Ripley ". . . one of the . . . outstanding cultural events connected with Washington in this century," the Hirshhorn gift is a resplendent example of one man's passion for art. Committed to major developments in painting and sculpture, the collection is international in scope.

More than 2,000 pieces of sculpture range from antiquity to the work of today's young creators. European and American examples from the 19th and 20th centuries are a focal point. More than one hundred of these, including such world-famous pieces as Rodin's *The Burghers of Calais;* Matisse's four bas-reliefs, *The Back;* and Moore's *King and Queen* will be on view in the Museum's open court along the walks bordering the reflecting pool of the sculpture garden.

The painting collection, comprising over 4,000 works, focuses on the current century. From the works of precursors such as Thomas Eakins and Winslow Homer to the canvases of the 1960s, the course of modern painting in America is covered in depth.

Complementing the United States section is a strong selection of paintings by modern European masters of the past three decades.

Because of the size and range of its collections, the Hirshhorn Museum will permit the study and exhibition of many major artists in a manner rarely possible elsewhere. Eakins, Gorky, DeKooning, Matisse, Moore, Miro, and Giacometti are among the outstanding artists represented by large holdings in the permanent collection.

The Gift

Joseph H. Hirshhorn's original gift to the Nation of some 6,000 paintings and sculptures was formally accepted by President Lyndon B. Johnson in a White House ceremony on May 17, 1966. In March 1972 a further gift of 166 sculptures and paintings was announced.

The Building

Congress authorized construction of the Museum and Sculpture Garden in November 1966, and ground was broken in January 1969.

For the site, architect Gordon Bunshaft designed a three-story cylindrical building 231 feet in diameter and raised 14 feet above a plaza on four massive sculptural supports. The exterior surface is a concrete and crushed granite aggregate. An inner sculpture court, 115 feet in diameter, encircles a bronze fountain.

The top floor is reserved for art research facilities and administrative offices. The other two above-ground floors, connected by escalators and elevators to the glass-enclosed lobby on the plaza level, are given over entirely to public galleries. Another public floor, below ground, consists of a large gallery for changing exhibits, a 280-seat auditorium, and a museum shop.

The Sculpture Garden

The sunken Sculpture Garden, enclosed by a wall of the same material as the Museum exterior, occupies a site 350 feet long and 140 feet wide between Jefferson and Adams Drives. A lower area in the center is enhanced by a reflecting pool.

National Gallery of Art

J. CARTER BROWN, Director

Mall entrance: North side at 6th Street, N.W.

Constitution Avenue entrance: at 6th Street, N.W.

Open: Daily except Christmas and New Year's Days

Hours: Weekdays—10:00 a.m. to 5:00 p.m. (9:00 p.m. in summer)
Sundays—12:00 noon to 9:00 p.m.

Telephone: (202) 737-4215

The National Gallery of Art maintains a permanent exhibition of masterworks by European and American artists and presents a continuing series of temporary exhibitions. It also sponsors lectures and concerts, and maintains its own orchestra. It administers fellowships for scholarly research and is constructing an East Building which will house, in addition to exhibitions of art, a Center for Advanced Study in the Visual Arts.

The National Gallery, although technically established as a bureau of the Smithsonian Institution, is an autonomous and separately administered organization and is governed by its own Board of Trustees

Comprehensive free guidebooks describing exhibits and services at the National Gallery of Art are available in the building, or by writing to: The Director, National Gallery of Art, Washington, D.C. 20565.

(ABOVE) Winslow Homer, *Bear Hunting-Prospect Rock.*

(RIGHT) Courtyard of building housing the National Collection of Fine Arts and the National Portrait Gallery.

HansHoffman, *Fermented Soil.*

National Collection of Fine Arts

JOSHUA C. TAYLOR, Director

G Street at 8th Street, N.W.
and
9th Street between F and G Streets, N.W.
(Note: Due to the continuing subway construction the G Street entrance may be temporarily closed.)

Open: Daily except Christmas Day

Hours: 10:00 a.m. to 5:30 p.m.

Telephone: (202) 381-5180

What's going on and where to find it

Information Desk
Located near the G Street entrance, with up-to-date information on special exhibits, lectures, and other activities.

Discussion Tours
Discussion Tours for school or adult groups, and *"Improvisation" Sessions* in the galleries for children may be arranged by calling the Education Department: 381-6541.

Prints and Drawings Study Room
Open Tuesday and Thursday afternoons and by appointment.

Works Not on Exhibition
Available for study by scholars on application.

Museum Shop
Near G Street entrance. On sale are NCFA publications, art books, posters, reproductions, and postcards.

Luncheon Facilities
Sandwiches and beverages are available on the first floor. In good weather the courtyard can be used for outdoor dining.

The National Collection of Fine Arts offers a panorama of painting, sculpture, and graphic art in the United States from the earliest times to the present. Its temporary exhibitions, accompanied by scholarly catalogues, explore in depth various aspects of this art.

Its Department of Education works with school programs and adult groups to make the Collection available to a wide public. The NCFA also coordinates and prepares exhibitions for circulation abroad in association with the United States Information Agency. Its *Bicentennial Inventory of American Painting Before 1914* is the first step in creating a computerized index of American works of art. The Conservation Laboratory that NCFA maintains jointly with the National Portrait Gallery also engages in research on artists' materials.

Eve Tempted. Marble,
by Hiram Powers (1805-1873).

Collections

Most prominent and many less well known artists of the United States are represented in the collections, which also include a small but rich group of works from other cultures. Early artists in America include Gustavus and John Hesselius, Benjamin West, and Gilbert Stuart. A large collection of miniatures extends from the early period through the course of American art. The more than four hundred paintings of Indians by George Catlin are from the collection he showed in Paris in the 1840s. Many fine examples of 19th-century sculpture complement the group of works from Hiram Powers' studio in Florence, left there at his death in 1873. Albert Pinkham Ryder is represented by a large and choice group of his works, as are the painters usually referred to as "American Impressionists." The various trends of 20th-century painting and sculpture—from the lively commentaries of Bellows and Glackens to the imposing paintings of Kline, Rauschenberg, and Gene Davis and the sculptures of Calder and Rickey—are all represented. The contemporary collection has been much advanced by the extensive gifts of the S. C. Johnson & Company and by gifts from other patrons and from artists.

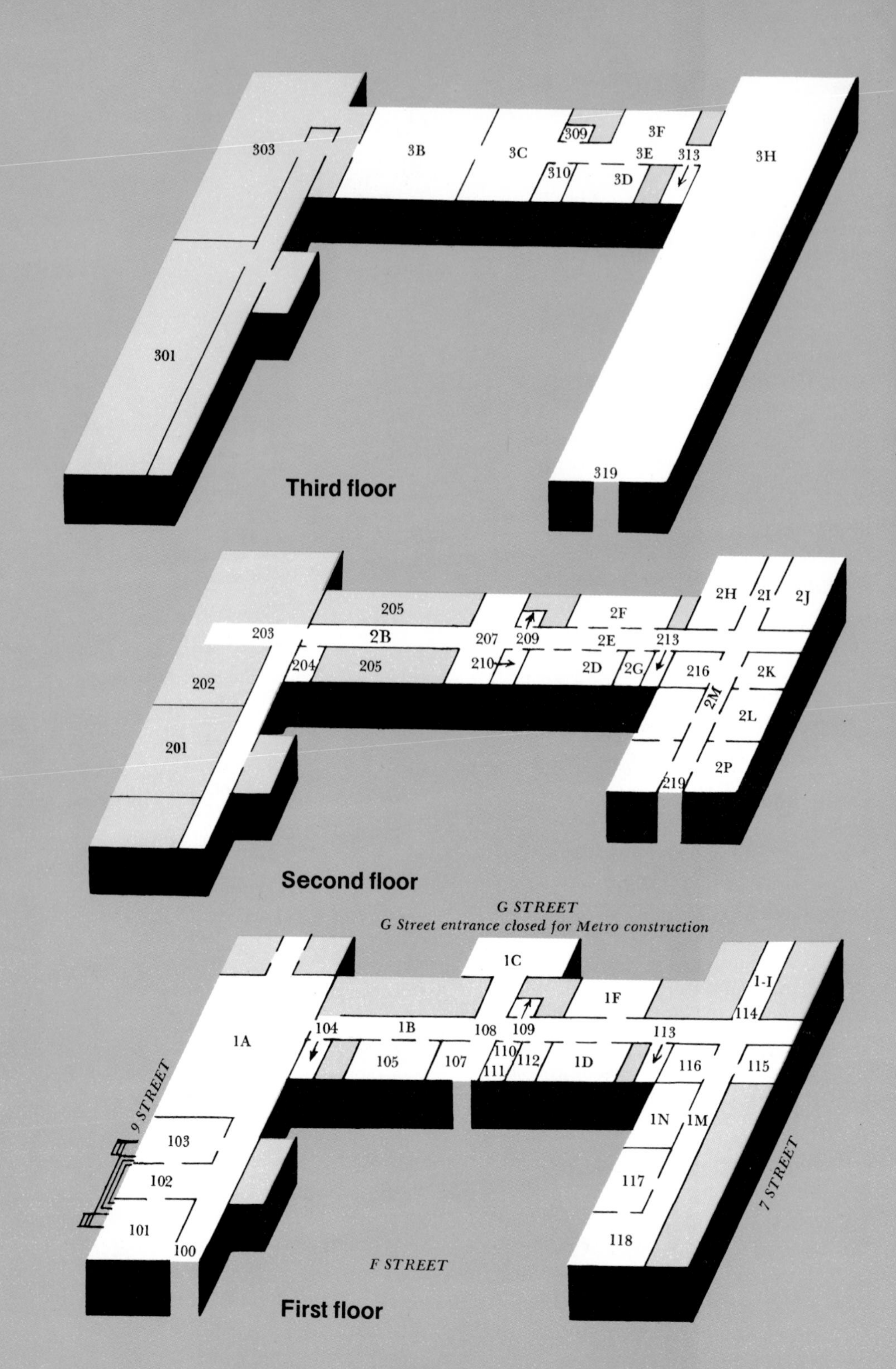

NATIONAL COLLECTION OF FINE ARTS

FIRST FLOOR

Galleries

1A	Granite Gallery
1A, 1B	Prints and Drawings Galleries
1C	Recent Acquisitions
1D	Children's Gallery
1F	"Discover" Gallery
1M, 1N	Galleries of European and Asiatic Art

Events and Services

102	Checkroom Lockers
118	Coffee Shop
103	David E. Finley Conference Room
114	Education Offices
109	Elevators
102	Entrance, 9th St.
108	Exit to F St. via Courtyard
100	Exit to National Portrait Gallery
102	Guard Station
102, 108	Information Desk
101	Lecture Hall (Films)
112	Museum Shop
105	Print and Drawing Study Room (Open Tuesday and Thursday afternoons and by appointment)
115	Public Affairs Office
108	Recent Acquisitions
	Rest Rooms
104	Men
113	Women
117	Smithsonian Associates Lounge (For Associates members only)
107	Smoking Lounge
110, 116	Stairs
111	Telephones
102	Wheelchairs

SECOND FLOOR

Galleries

2B	Washington Painters
2D	Winslow Homer and Albert Pinkham Ryder
2E, 2F	19th-Century Landscape
2G	American Miniatures
2H	Temporary Exhibitions
2I	Painters and Sculptors in Italy
2J	Hiram Powers
2K	John Rogers Groups
2L	Lafarge and End-of-Century
2M	Painters in Paris and Munich
2N, 2O	American "Impressionists"
2P	Dewing and Thayer

Events and Services

201	Conservation Lab.
209	Elevators
219	Exit to National Portrait Gallery
203, 205	Offices, Administrative and Curatorial
202	Photography Lab.
203	Receptionist
	Rest Rooms
213	Men
204	Women
207	Smoking Lounge
210, 216	Stairs

THIRD FLOOR

Galleries

3B	Temporary Exhibitions
3C	Sculpture Lounge
3E, 3F	Contemporary Painting and Sculpture
3D	Irene & Herbert F. Johnson Gallery
3H	Lincoln Gallery Selections from the Permanent Collection 18th Century to the Present

Events and Services

309	Elevators
301	Library
303	Research Offices
	Rest Rooms
313	Men
310	Stairs
319	Exit to National Portrait Gallery

George Catlin, *Four Bears.*

Agnes Tait, *Winter Afternoon, Central Park, 1934.*

The historic Lincoln Gallery *(3-H)* on the third floor of the east wing is an appropriate place to start a tour of the collection. In this immense hall, where once was held the reception celebrating Lincoln's second inaugural, is now displayed a sampling of works in the permanent collection, 18th-century to the present. Also on that floor are galleries of contemporary paintings and sculpture *(3-C, E, F)* including works from the *S. C. Johnson Collection (3-D),* and a gallery *(3-B)* devoted to major special exhibitions.

Lincoln Gallery displaying a sampling of American art, 18th century to present.

School children on "Improvisational Tour" respond to *Green Diagonal,* acrylic painting by Alexander Liberman.

On the second floor are works of 19th-century artists, with galleries devoted to groups such as landscapists *(2-E, F)* and miniaturists *(2-G),* as well as to such individuals as Winslow Homer *(2-D),* Hiram

Richard Lytle, *The Cave.*

Powers *(2-J),* and Albert Pinkham Ryder *(2-D).*

An architecturally interesting stairway in the east wing leads to the first-floor area of the Education Department, where a print workshop is maintained, in conjunction with area schools, and a gallery for the exhibition of student work. Among the other galleries on this floor are the Children's Gallery *(1-D),* offering young visitors an introduction to art and creative perception; the Discover Gallery *(1-F),* with its special exhibitions on various aspects of art; the Granite Gallery *(1-A)* in the west wing, which houses a rotating exhibition of prints and drawings from the collection; and the Corridor Gallery *(1-B),* which presents temporary special exhibitions of the graphic arts.

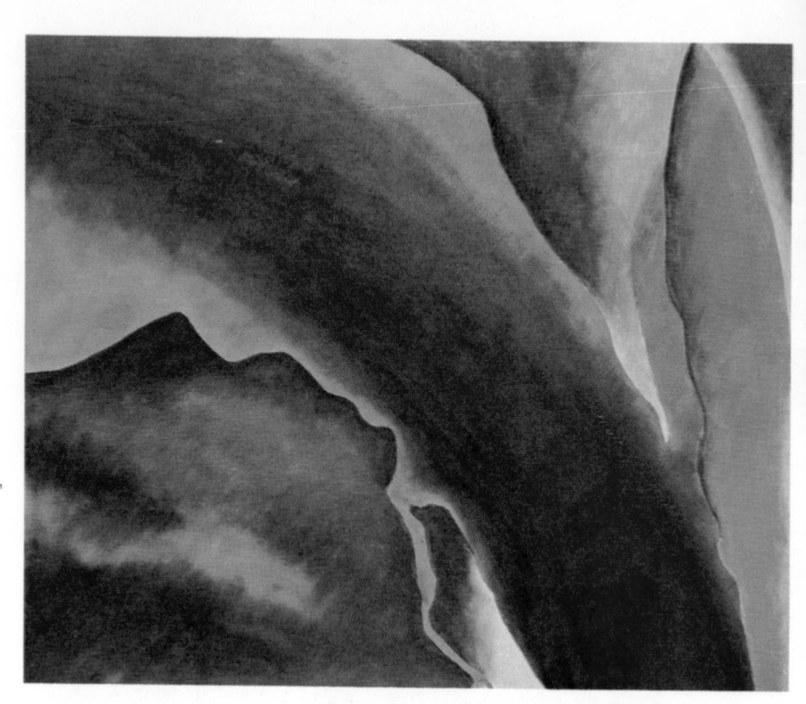

Georgia O'Keefe,
Only One.

History

The National Collection traces its beginning to the 1846 Act of Establishment, in which the Congress directed the Smithsonian to maintain a museum and an art gallery. In the early days, exploration of the West and widespread interest in the natural sciences largely absorbed the Smithsonian's funds and energies, so that although some of the art works to which it fell heir antedate the Institution itself, not until the 1890s, under Samuel P. Langley, was the Institution able to take effective steps to build up the collection.

The efforts of Secretary Langley led to the gift by Harriet Lane Johnston, niece of President James Buchanan, of her collection of paintings to a national gallery, should one be established. The designation in 1906 of the Smithsonian's collections as the National Gallery of Art assured it the Johnston collection; and in 1907, from William T. Evans, came another large group of paintings.

During the period 1907-1957 a steady, if slow, growth of the Gallery was maintained by gifts of works of art, or funds for their purchase, by Henry Ward Ranger, Ralph Cross Johnson, John Gellatly, and others.

Because no separate building in the Smithsonian group on the Mall was available, the growing collection was allotted a hall in the Natural History Building when it opened in 1909. As that became overcrowded, the works of art were either stored or lent to government offices throughout Washington.

In 1937, when Andrew Mellon's great gift of art to the Nation was designated the National Gallery of Art, the older collection was renamed the National

(LEFT) Albert P. Ryder, *Moonlight.*

(BELOW) Thomas Moran, *Grand Canyon of the Yellowstone.*

Collection of Fine Arts. At that time a move was made to house it in a modern gallery, for the design of which Eero Saarinen won a $25,000 award, but progress was halted by the onset of war.

In the late 1950s, however, the old Patent Office Building (see p. 115) was turned over to the Smithsonian for renovation and restoration as a home for the National Collection, for the newly formed National Portrait Gallery, and, later, for the Archives of American Art. In this magnificently proportioned "Greek Revival" building dating from the early days of the Republic, it was finally possible to display appropriately the wealth of art accumulated in the collection, and to acquire representative examples of the work produced by this country's varied and vital art community.

The Patent Office Building housing the National Collection of Fine Arts and the National Portrait Gallery.

The "Lansdowne" portrait of George Washington, painted by Gilbert Stuart, hanging at the entrance to the Presidential Corridor.

(RIGHT) Edwin Booth,
Thomas Hicks.

National Portrait Gallery

MARVIN S. SADIK, Director

F Street at 8th St., N.W.
Open: Daily except Christmas
Hours: 10:00 a.m. to 5:30 p.m.
Telephone: (202) 628-4422

What's going on and where to find it

Information Desk
Located inside the main entrance, with up-to-date information on special exhibits, lectures, and other activities.

Guided Tours
For information on regular and Drop-In Tours, call 628-4422.

Museum Shop
A Smithsonian Bookstore specializes in art and history books and posters, including catalogues issued by the National Portrait Gallery for special exhibitions such as *Portraits of the American Stage 1771-1971*, and *If Elected . . . Unsuccessful Candidates for the Presidency 1796-1968.*

Pocahontas.
Unidentified artist.

The National Portrait Gallery was established for the exhibition of portraits and statuary of men and women who have made significant contributions to the history, development, and culture of the people of the United States. The Museum also honors the artists who created these images.

In this magnificent building, and in these settings that so enhance the portraits, the visitor comes face to face with personalities who have made American history for four centuries.

The Permanent Collection

The Gallery's primary goal is the formation of a permanent collection of portraits of notable figures, preferably taken directly from life, or at least contemporary with the subject, whenever possible. Portraits are not admitted to the permanent collection until ten years after the death of the subject. Under special circumstances, however, the Gallery may accept a portrait for later addition to the collection. The ultimate decision as to whose portraits shall be included in the permanent collection rests with the National Portrait Gallery Commission.

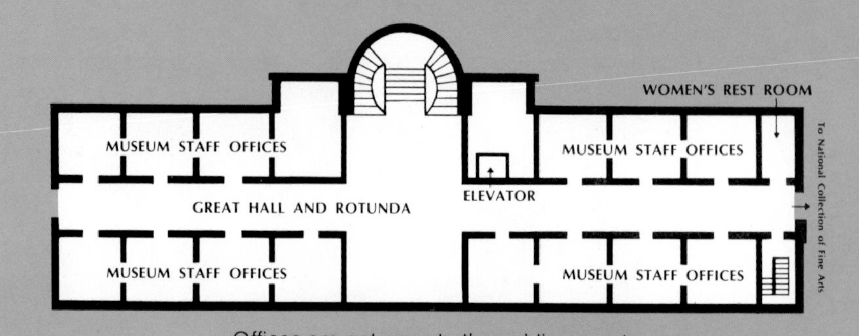

Offices are not open to the public except by specific appointment with staff member.

Third floor

Second floor

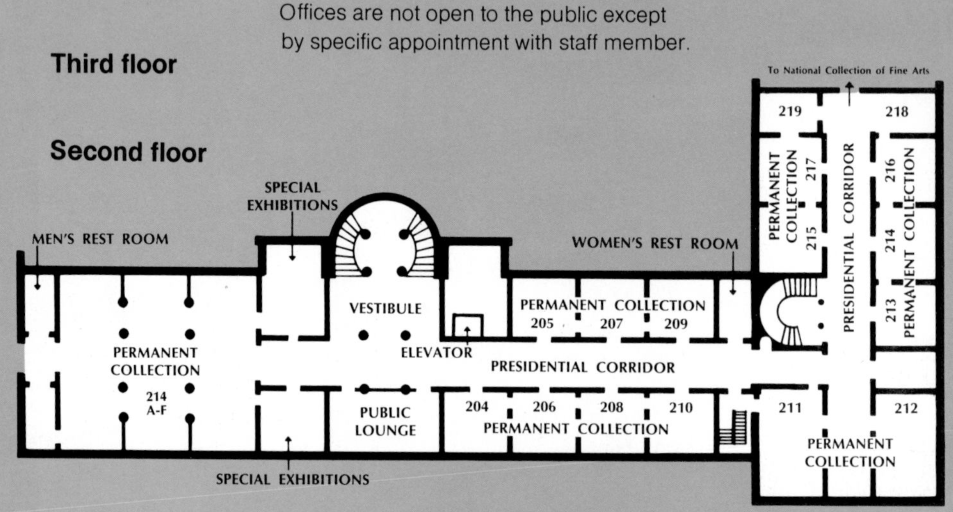

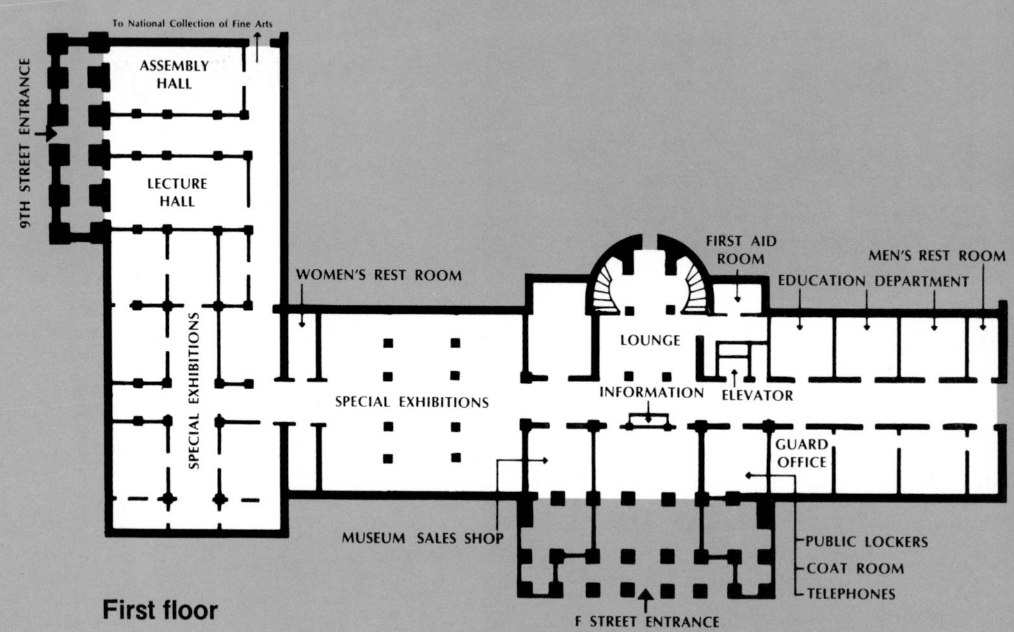

First floor

NATIONAL PORTRAIT GALLERY

FIRST FLOOR

To the left of the main entrance are galleries for special, temporary exhibits that augment and elaborate on the themes and purposes of the permanent collection.

Leading to the second floor is a gracefully curved double staircase at the foot of which hangs a portrait of Pocahontas painted by an unknown English artist.

SECOND FLOOR

The vestibule is dominated by a magnificent full-length portrait of George Washington by Gilbert Stuart, painted in 1796.
The open galleries on the west side of the building (numbered *214 a* through *f*) show a selection of portrait sculpture rotated from the permanent collection. The busts range from Benjamin Franklin to John Brown to Woodrow Wilson and from Sam Houston to Will Rogers.

Returning to the vestibule, the Presidential Corridor with its historic portraits of the presidents extends straight ahead and around the corner. At the eastern end, under the Presidential Seal, is the special alcove reserved for the present occupant of the White House. The 1968 portrait of President Nixon was painted by Norman Rockwell.

The exhibition of selected portraits from the permanent collection is shown in chronologically related groupings in the intimate galleries to the right and left of the Presidential Corridor. Each gallery displays eight to ten likenesses and each is accompanied by a brief historical essay. Many famous portraitists are represented in these galleries, among them John Singleton Copley, Benjamin West, Gilbert Stuart, Charles Willson Peale, Thomas Sully, John Singer Sargent and Augustus Saint-Gaudens.

Mary McLeod Bethune, Betsy Graves Reyneau.

Galleries 204-206-208-210
These show makers of the Nation from the 18th through the middle of the 19th centuries.

Galleries 211-212
Here are men and women connected with the causes and pursuits of the Civil War.

Gertrude Stein (1874-1946), author. By Jo Davidson, 1923.

George Washington, Rembrandt Peale.

Galleries 205-207-209
On the opposite side of the Presidential Corridor, these galleries continue the 19th century, with portraits of writers, philosophers, artists, and scientists of this period.

Galleries 213-214-216- and 215-217-219
These extend the march of American history through the latter part of the 19th century up to the present.

(From here the visitor has direct access to the second floor of the National Collection of Fine Arts.)

THIRD FLOOR

The third floor, with its Rotunda and Great Hall, is occupied by Gallery staff offices.

History

The first official gesture toward creating a national portrait gallery was made in 1857 when Congress commissioned G. P. A. Healy to paint a series of Presidential portraits for the White House. In the decades following World War I, a national portrait

(LEFT) Balconied Model Hall on third floor.

National Collection of Fine Arts and National Portrait Gallery library contains research facilities for scholars.

gallery was seriously proposed as a part of the general art collection then developing within the Smithsonian Institution. However, it was not until 1962 that the *National Portrait Gallery of the United States* was officially established by an Act of Congress, making it the fourth such gallery in the world and the first in the Western Hemisphere. It opened to the public in 1968 in its present quarters in the historic "Old Patent Office Building," which it shares with the National Collection of Fine Arts.

Building

Located midway between the Capitol and the White House, the "Old Patent Office Building," now shared by the National Collection of Fine Arts, the National Portrait Gallery and the Archives of American Art, is one of the noblest examples of monumental "Greek Revival" architecture in this country. It was designed in 1836; only the White House and the Capitol are older and can approach it in beauty.

In the historic Lincoln Gallery on the third floor, an astonishing hall nearly 300 feet long, with 32 marble pillars supporting an airy, elegant vaulted ceiling, 4,000 people gathered for Abraham Lincoln's second inaugural ball just five weeks before his assassination in 1865. Just a few years earlier, during the Civil War, the building was pressed into service as a makeshift hospital and it was here that wounded troops were nursed by a Patent Office copyist named Clara Barton—later the founder of the American Red Cross.

Surviving a devastating fire in 1877, the building was rebuilt and served over the next eighty years to house the Patent Office and other federal offices. An attempt to raze the building to provide downtown parking in the mid-1950s was thwarted by President Eisenhower and Congressional leaders. The decision was made by Congress to permit the building to house its present dual art collections in 1958; in 1964 renovation began, and in 1968 the National Portrait Gallery and the National Collection of Fine Arts took occupancy.

Octagon Room.

Palm Court.

Renwick Gallery

LLOYD E. HERMAN, Administrator

Pennsylvania Avenue at 17th Street, N.W.
Open: Daily except Christmas
Hours: 10:00 a.m. to 5:30 p.m.
Telephone: (202) 628-4422

(OPPOSITE PAGE) Grand Salon.

(RIGHT) Upper Hall, looking across to Octagon Room.

"Dedicated to art" . . .

The Renwick Gallery, a department of the National Collection of Fine Arts, presents in its galleries special exhibitions on American design and crafts. These include inquiries into the nature of design, retrospective surveys of architecture and crafts, and the work of outstanding American craftsmen. One of its galleries displays works from abroad, and its carefully restored Second Empire Grand Salon of the 1870s offers the visitor the chance to savor an art museum of that period.

Not only the Grand Salon, but also the entrance foyer, the grand staircase, the corridors, and another principal room—the Octagon Room—have been restored and furnished to reflect the taste of the period in which they were created (1860-75), and are among the handsomest interiors in Washington.

The Grand Salon was the main picture gallery when the building housed the Corcoran art collection, and on its walls now hang many of the paintings displayed there almost a century ago, on loan from the Corcoran Gallery of Art. The Octagon Room was originally intended to display the Corcoran's most important work of statuary, Hiram Powers' *The Greek Slave.* The restoration and furnishing of the room have been generously supported by the Morris and Gwendolyn Cafritz Foundation.

View of the stairway between first and second floors.

Building

The building itself is an historic work, and its restoration is in part a result of the effort to preserve the character of the Lafayette Park-Pennsylvania Avenue area across from the White House.

It was designed in 1859 by James Renwick, Jr. to house the art collection of William W. Corcoran, but construction was interrupted by the Civil War. The unfinished building was used for military purposes until 1869. and was finally completed in 1874. It served as Washington's first extensive art museum until 1897, when the Corcoran collection was removed to the present, larger Corcoran Gallery a few blocks away.

From 1899 to 1964 the building housed the U.S. Court of Claims. When it was turned over to the Smithsonian in 1966 to be restored and used for exhibitions, it was renamed the Renwick Gallery in honor of its architect. It was opened to the public in January 1972.

Its design, known in the 1850s as "French Renaissance," is today commonly referred to as "Second Empire" style. The two-story building, with basement, measures 106 by 126 feet. Constructed of red brick with sandstone facings and ornaments, it has a slate mansard roof capped on the three outer corners with pavilions topped with iron crestings. The capitals of the pilasters on its face take the form of Indian corn, and over the front entrance appears Corcoran's monogram and a profile portrait, with the motto "Dedicated to Art," and additional decorations representing architecture and music.

John F. Kennedy Center for the Performing Arts

Rock Creek Parkway at New Hampshire Avenue and F Street, N.W.
Telephone: (202) 254-3774

What's going on and where to find it

Information Desks
Located in the Hall of Nations, Hall of States, and Motor Lobby A.

Free Guided Tours
Conducted through the three theaters (when rehearsal and production schedules permit), and to the majority of areas where foreign gifts are located. For information, call 254-3600.

Parking
Pay parking is available in the Kennedy Center garage and in the nearby Watergate and Columbia Plaza garages. (Thirty minutes of free parking is provided in the Kennedy Center garage for patrons purchasing tickets at the box offices from 10:00 until 6:00 weekdays; noon until 6:00 Sundays. Parking tickets must be validated at the box office.)

Box Offices

Open:	10:00 a.m. to 9:00 p.m. weekdays	
	Noon to 9:00 p.m. Sundays	
Telephones:	Concert Hall Ticket Office	254-3776
	Eisenhower Theater Ticket Office	254-3670
	Opera House Ticket Office	254-3770

Created in 1958 by Congressional Act as the National Cultural Center and designated in 1964 as a memorial to the late President, the John F. Kennedy Center for the Performing Arts was directed by Congress to:

—Present classical and contemporary music, opera, drama, dance, and poetry from this and other countries;

—Present lectures and other programs;

—Develop programs in the above arts for all age groups, designed specifically for their participation, education, and recreation.

Administered by the National Park Service, the Kennedy Center, designed by architect Edward Durell Stone, stands on a 17-acre tract along the east bank of the Potomac, on the edge of Georgetown in northwest Washington. Groundbreaking took place in December 1964 and the Center opened officially on September 8, 1971, with the world premiere of Leonard Bernstein's *Mass* in the Opera House.

The building, 630 feet long and 300 feet wide, is faced with Carrara marble. Three magnificent theaters occupy the main level: the Opera House seats 2,200; the more intimate 1,100-seat Eisenhower Theater is next to it on the north side; the 2,750-seat Concert Hall on the south. Connecting them is the red-carpeted, marble-walled Grand Foyer, facing the River Terrace. Extending the entire length of the building, the Foyer is lit by eighteen crystal chandeliers, its dominant feature a giant sculptured head in bronze of President Kennedy.

Above the theaters, on the Roof Terrace level, three restaurants provide panoramic views of the city and an opportunity for outdoor dining. This floor will eventually contain the Film Theater and an exhibition and reception area.

Beneath the building, parking facilities accommodate 1,500 cars.

As an independently administered bureau of the Smithsonian, the Kennedy Center is governed by its own board of trustees, of which the Secretary of the Smithsonian is an ex-officio member.

(RIGHT) Great Flight Cage.

(BELOW) Bird House.

(RIGHT) Orangutan infant, *Melati.*

National Zoological Park

THEODORE H. REED, Director

Entrances: Connecticut Avenue, N.W.
(3000 block between Cathedral Avenue and Devonshire Street)
Harvard Street and Adams Mill Road intersection
Beach Drive in Rock Creek Park

Open: Daily

Hours: *Gates*—Open at 6:00 a.m.
Entrance gates close when buildings close; exit gates close one hour later.
Buildings—Open at 9:00 a.m.
Close 4:30 p.m. during winter months; 6:00 p.m. in warmer months

Telephone: (202) 628-4422

What's going on and where to find it

(Numbers in parentheses refer to map, pp. 128 and 129)

Bus Routes
Connecticut Avenue entrance served by L2 and L4 buses; H2 bus stops at the Harvard Street entrance.

Parking
Parking lots are located near the Connecticut Avenue, Harvard Street, and Beach Drive entrances; at the Elephant House; along Rock Creek; and behind the cafeteria. Charge: $1.00 per day. Buses must park behind the Zoo cafeteria in spaces reserved for buses only. (See map.)

Cafeteria (32) **and Picnic Facilities** (33)
The Zoo cafeteria is open daily, with hours corresponding to those of the other Zoo buildings. In the summer months, a snack bar operates on the upper level of the Panda House. An outdoor picnic terrace adjoins the cafeteria and other picnic tables are to be found throughout the Zoo grounds.

Visiting Groups and Tours
No advance arrangements are necessary for visiting groups, who are welcome at any time. (Non-ambulatory groups should make prior arrangements several days in advance by calling Zoo Police, (202) 381-7231.)

Guided tours provided by volunteers of the Friends of the National Zoo are available by reservation. From mid-March through May, reservations should be made a month in advance. Call 232-7703 for information on tours and reservations.

Services
The Zoo's police station is located next to the cafeteria (31).
It offers:

- —First aid
- —Lost and found service
- —Use of wheelchairs
- —Refuge for lost children (Keepers in each building also assist in locating lost persons)
- —Rest rooms

(See map for other locations.)

Train Rides
Trackless trains circulate through the grounds from April 1 through October 31 at a nominal charge. Operated by the Friends of the National Zoo, the trains stop at the Bird House (5), the Elephant House (11), and Cafeteria (32). Ticket holders may reboard at no extra charge.

Gift Shop (34)
Operated by Friends of the National Zoo, the gift shop is located near the big clock at the Lion House concourse. It has a variety of unusual zoo-oriented articles for sale, as well as film souvenirs, balloons, and post cards. Special animal food can also be purchased.

Feeding Times
Feeding schedules are as follows:

Monkey House—9:30 and 2:30
Lion House—1:30 (except Sundays)
Beaver Valley—1:30
Wolves and wild dogs—1:30
Bears—8:30 and 3:00
Elephant House—3:00
Sea lions—8:45 and 3:15
Birds—Fed throughout the day
Pandas—10:00 and 4:00

Please honor requests not to feed specified animals.

Some rules to follow, please . . .

- —Personal pets are not allowed in the Zoo—on leashes or otherwise. Visitors traveling with pets are permitted to leave their animals safely locked in their cars on the Zoo grounds, provided the pets are left with adequate ventilation, and water, if necessary.
- —Help keep the Zoo clean by using the trash containers.
- —Always stay on your side of the guardrails.
- —Take all the photographs you wish in public areas, but not behind guardrails.

NATIONAL ZOOLOGICAL PARK

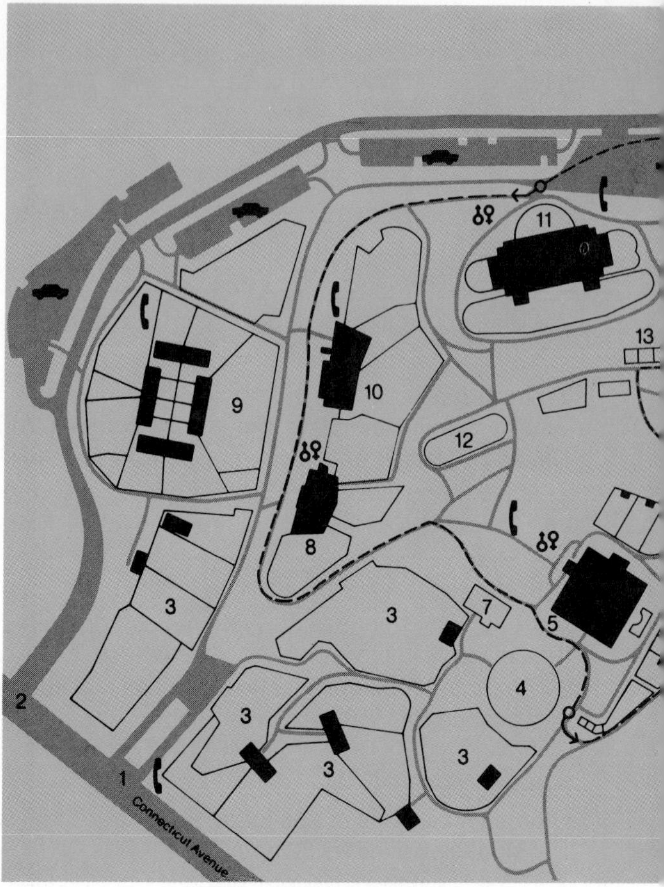

1 Connecticut Avenue pedestrian entrance

2 Connecticut Avenue vehicular entrance

3 Deer areas and bongos

Axis deer	Pere David's deer
Sika deer	White-tailed deer
Reindeer	Brow-antlered deer

4 Great flight cage

5 Bird House

6 Ostrich, pheasant & crane line

7 Eagles and vultures

8 Delicate-hoofed stock building
- Greater kudus
- Dorcas gazelles
- Scimitar-horned oryx

9 Hardy-hoofed stock complex
- Zebras
- Wildebeests
- Cape buffaloes

10 Panda House
- Giant Pandas

11 Elephant House
- African & Asian elephants
- African & Indian rhinoceroses
- Nile & pygmy hippopotamuses
- Giraffes

12 Birds

13 Hawks and owls

14 Llamas, pygmy goats, kangaroos

15 Small Mammal & Great Ape Building
- Gorillas and orangutans

16 Lesser pandas

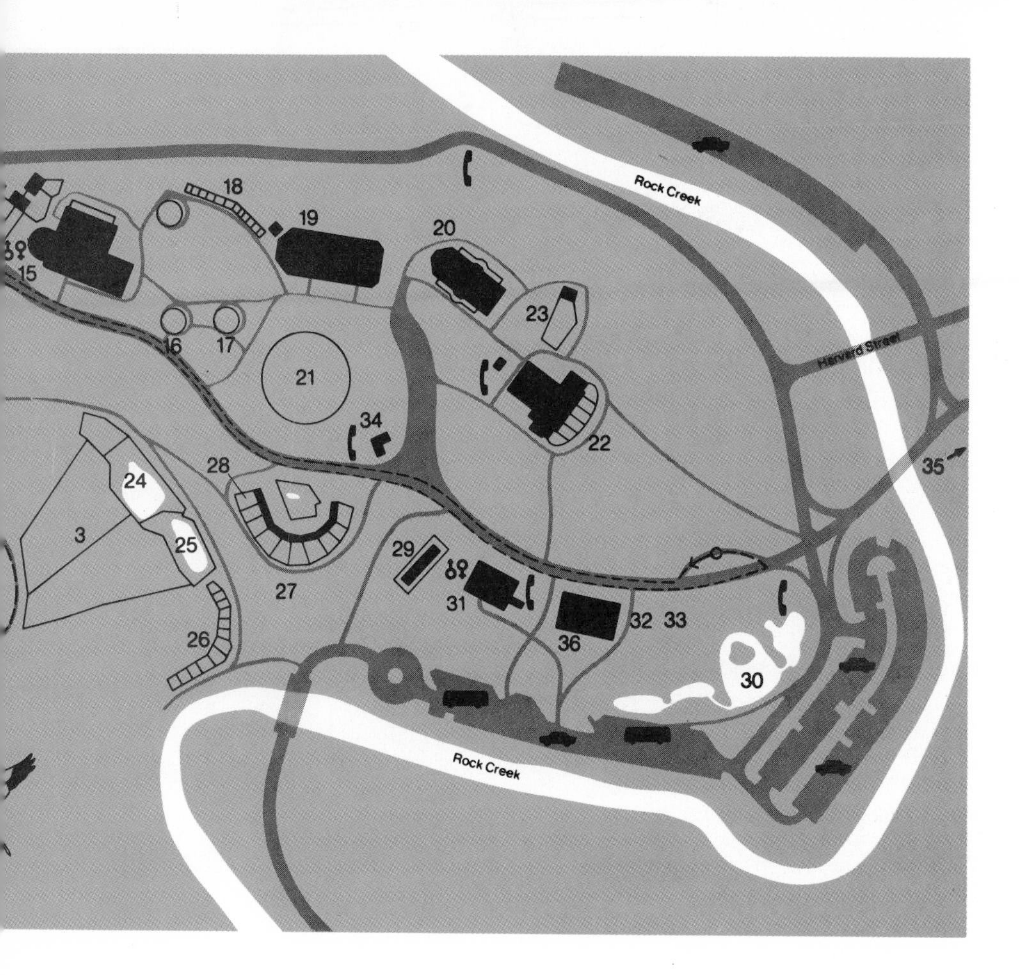

17 Prairie dogs

18 Bears and monkeys

19 Reptile House

20 Monkey House

21 Tortoise yard

22 Lion House
   Large cats

23 Cheetah run

24 Tapir yard

25 Sea lion pool

26 Wolves, foxes & wild dogs

27 Bears

Kodiak	European brown
Polar	Sloth
Grizzly	Hybrids

28 Smokey Bear

29 Small hardy cats

30 Waterfowl yards

31 Police Station—Restrooms—First Aid

32 Cafeteria

33 Picnic area

34 Gift Shop

35 Rock Creek Parkway entrance

36 Friends of the National Zoo
   Office, basement of cafeteria

Telephone

Restrooms

Trackless Train

Parking

Great Flight Cage.

zoo/zü/n. -s [short for *zoological garden*] 1: a zoological garden or collection of living animals usually for public display

A concise definition, according to Webster, but one which hardly conveys the fun in store for the entire family in

The National Zoological Park

Located on 165 acres in the heart of Washington's Rock Creek Park, the Zoo welcomes millions of visitors each year. On exhibit are 2,500 animals of about 800 different species. There are 400 kinds of birds, 200 kinds of mammals, and 200 kinds of reptiles and amphibians.

In addition, the Zoo plays a significant role in research to increase man's knowledge of animals and to help in preserving the many species throughout the world which are threatened with extinction.

The map on pp. 128 and 129 will help you find your way around and decide on what you want to see. Information on other things you may want to know more about follows.

Buildings

Several buildings have been constructed recently as part of the modernization program at the Zoo.

Elephants.

(TOP OF PAGE) Lesser panda.

These include the *Bird House,* with an unusual free-flight room through which visitors may walk while the birds fly about overhead.

Near the Bird House is the graceful and artistic *Great Flight Cage.* With a 90-foot high mast, it is constructed with six slender parabolic steel arches, supporting a tent of vinyl-covered wire. Visitors enter through double sets of glass doors and stroll among boulders, waterfalls, and pools, with no physical barrier between them and the free-flying birds.

In the same area are the *Panda House* and a building for delicate-hoofed stock.

Other major buildings are the *Elephant House,* the *Small Mammal House,* the *Reptile House,* the *Monkey House,* and the *Lion House,* which is the oldest of the Zoo buildings. Completed in 1891, this structure was used originally to provide shelter for any animal that needed warm winter quarters. Now it houses the Zoo's collection of large cats.

Outdoor enclosures for monkeys and small cats are near the Lion House. Dens and cages for the large bears are across the street. In a valley below the bear dens there are a sea lion pool, enclosures for the wild dogs, and the tapir yard.

Ling-Ling.

Notable Residents

As the Nation's "official zoo," the National Zoological Park is host to delegations of visitors from foreign countries and the recipient of donations of rare animals.

Certainly the most famous recent gifts have been Ling-Ling and Hsing-Hsing (pronounced Shing-Shing), presented by the People's Republic of China to the United States in 1972. From their arrival at the Zoo on an April morning, the two giant pandas have attracted millions of visitors who delight in their amusing ways. Ling-Ling, the female, is the larger, older, and more aggressive of the two. She is a playful extrovert and considered a "clown" by her keepers and her audience. If you're lucky you may see her taking a bath in her wooden tub, or rummaging around in her bamboo pot, getting dirty and nibbling her favorite food at the same time. Hsing-Hsing exhibits male conservatism in contrast to Ling-Ling's antics, spending much of his solitary time lying in his air-conditioned enclosure. The two pandas are being

(ABOVE, AND TOP OF PAGE) Ling-Ling.

kept separate until both are older and more mature when it is planned they will meet, and eventually mate. Their diet is largely gruel and bamboo, apples and bananas, and for Ling-Ling, carrots.

Other famous animals donated by other countries in recent years include Mohini, a rare white tigress from India; two Komodo monitor lizards (commonly called "Komodo dragons") from Indonesia; and kiwis from New Zealand.

Celebrated natives of the United States are Smokey Bear, the living symbol of forest-fire prevention and wildlife conservation, and Ham, the chimpanzee who made a 16-minute space capsule voyage in 1961.

Vanishing Animals

The National Zoological Park is dedicated to the preservation of all endangered species. Throughout the Zoo the endangered animal symbol—a bovine skull with the words *Vanishing Animal* superimposed—is

used to designate those animals in the collection whose numbers are seriously diminishing in the wild.

Among them are:
Orangutan
Polar bear
Great Indian rhino
Pygmy hippopotamus
Golden marmoset
Syrian brown bear
Grizzly bear
American alligator
Hawaiian goose
Galapagos tortoise
Lion-tailed macaque
Parma wallaby

(TOP OF PAGE) Mohini Rewa.

(ABOVE LEFT) Offspring of Mohini Rewa, rare white tigress from India, with many friends.

(ABOVE RIGHT) Smokey Bear.

(LEFT) Ham.

(ABOVE)
Polar bear.

(LEFT)
Golden marmosets.

(BELOW LEFT)
Galapagos tortoise.

(BELOW RIGHT)
Pygmy hippo.

Friends of the National Zoo

A membership organization devoted to educational and charitable purposes, *Friends of the National Zoo* is dedicated to informing the public on matters relating to the increase and improvement of the facilities and collection of the National Zoological Park. It encourages the Zoo's use by the general public and the schools for educational purposes.

History

The Zoo was established in 1889 by Congress, at the urging of the third Secretary of the Smithsonian, Samuel Pierpont Langley, who was concerned with saving the American bison from extinction at a time when this species was on the verge of being wiped out.

Six bison and other animals belonging to the Smithsonian were kept in enclosures behind the "Castle" on the Mall until the facilities at the Zoo were ready.

By 1926 the collection numbered 1,700 individuals. That same year the collection was nearly doubled by the addition of 1,353 animals brought back by the Smithsonian-Chrysler Expedition from what is now Kenya. In 1937 the National Geographic-Smithsonian Expedition to the East Indies added another 879 specimens. The year 1939 found Zoo personnel in southern Asia, and with Admiral Byrd in the Antarctic, collecting more rare animals. The Smithsonian-Firestone Expedition to Liberia in 1940 supplied still more.

These expeditions, gifts from individuals and foreign governments, and exchanges with other zoos have all contributed to the Zoo's steady growth.

Research

In recent years, the Zoo has sponsored and participated in ecological programs in many parts of the world concerned with the study of animals in their natural environments and the study of habitats. In addition, various research projects have been carried out which have contributed to the knowledge of the biology and behavior of exotic mammals.

A new animal hospital and scientific research building (not open to the public) was constructed at the Zoo recently.

Bison at the "Castle," late 19th century.

NOTE: More views of Hsing-Hsing and Ling-Ling inside back fold-out.

An innovative experiment in public education . . .

This capsule museum in a converted movie theater is operated in close cooperation between the Smithsonian and the local community. Located in Southeast Washington in the historic section called Anacostia, the Museum seeks actively to broaden the horizon of the community, serving as both an exhibits center and an educational center responsive to the needs of the local inhabitants.

Its special exhibits, developed in cooperation with an advisory committee of neighborhood residents, have dealt with such subjects as: "This Is Africa," presenting traditional and contemporary African art; "The Sage of Anacostia, 1817-1895" on the life and times of Frederick Douglass, a former slave who became a noted journalist, orator, and abolitionist; "This Thing Called Jazz," featuring live demonstrations, recordings, artifacts, and an environmental room putting the viewer in the middle of a simulated New Orleans jazz parade. The District of Columbia Art Association exhibits annually. Increasingly, special emphasis is placed on urban problems and methods of dealing with them. "The Evolution of a Community" was based on materials gathered by the Center for Anacostia Studies, which was established by the Museum to help

Anacostia Neighborhood Museum

JOHN R. KINARD, Director

2405 Martin Luther King, Jr. Avenue, S.E.
Open: Daily except Christmas
Hours: Weekdays—10:00 a.m. to 6:00 p.m.
Saturday and Sunday—1:00 to 6:00 p.m.
Telephone: (202) 678-1200

the community place its current problems in historical perspective, thus enabling the residents to move with more understanding toward solutions.

The Museum's educational programs involve the neighborhood, particularly its young people, in projects that increase their skills and expand their understanding of the society around them. Certain exhibits are extended to the playgrounds, schools, and churches of Anacostia.

In these ways the Anacostia Neighborhood Museum assures a fresh, non-traditional approach to the role of the museum generally.

Visitors in the children's room.

*A look into the past . . .
and the future*

Founded in 1895 by the Hewitt sisters, granddaughters of New York manufacturer and philanthropist Peter Cooper, the Cooper Union Museum for the Arts and Decoration served throughout this century as a center for the study of historical and contemporary design. Faced with discontinuance in the early 1960s because of lack of space and financial problems, the Museum was saved by a major fund-raising drive by its supporters, combined with its transfer from the Cooper Union for the Advancement of Science and Art—a tuition-free educational institution—to the Smithsonian in 1968.

At that time its present name was adopted and arrangements were made to house the collections in the Andrew Carnegie mansion, a Fifth Avenue landmark since it was built in 1901 at a cost of a million-and-a-half dollars. In 1972 the property was given to the Smithsonian by the Carnegie Corporation. Renovation of the 64-room Victorian mansion now in progress will assure its function as a magnificent background for the display of products of international design activity, as well as the processes by

Cooper-Hewitt Museum of the Decorative Arts and Design

LISA M. TAYLOR, Director

9 East 90th Street, New York, N.Y. 10028
(Fifth Avenue between 90th and 91st Streets)
Telephone: (212) 860-2011

Opening scheduled for 1975

which objects assume their forms and the ways in which design affects our lives.

Expected to open during 1974, the new Cooper-Hewitt Museum will feature changing exhibitions derived from its own collections and others and will retain its position as a permanent study center. The renovated mansion will contain workshops; conservation and photographic laboratories; a children's environment center; a media center; a flexible, multipurpose theater; a restaurant overlooking Central Park; and a museum shop.

The Collections

Of a scope and quality unequalled in this country, the Cooper-Hewitt collection consists of more than 85,000 decorative arts items. Major parts are textiles, drawings, prints, wallpaper, metalwork, woodwork, and furniture. These elements are particularly strong in objects representing the 17th through the 19th centuries and are being expanded to include contemporary works and urban and industrial designs. The library contains some 13,000 volumes, of which nearly 2,000 are rare books.

If you want to know more about the Smithsonian...

you may want to consult these books about it.

Hellman, Geoffrey T.
The Smithsonian: Octopus on the Mall. 224 pp. New York City: J. B. Lippincott. 1967.

Karp, Walter.
The Smithsonian Institution: An Establishment for the Increase and Diffusion of Knowledge among Men. 125 pp., illus. Washington, D.C.: The Smithsonian Institution and American Heritage, 1965.

Oehser, Paul H.
The Smithsonian Institution. Foreword by S. Dillon Ripley. In Praeger Library of U.S. Government Departments and Agencies. xii-275 pp., illus. New York: Praeger Publishers, 1970.

Index

The following persons were of invaluable assistance in the preparation of this book:

Maureen R. Jacoby

Virginia M. Fleischman

John S. Lea

Russell Bourne

Allan Stone

William Craig

Frank Grohowski

Doris C. O'Neill

Murray Benson, *Publisher*

Photo credits:

Lee Boltin
Barbara Fahs Charles
Evening Star Photo by Arthur Ellis
Irving Haberman
Robert Lautman
Francine Schroeder
Pat Vosburgh
Office of Printing and Photograhic Services

Notes

254 3600

Parking 1:15 45 minutes

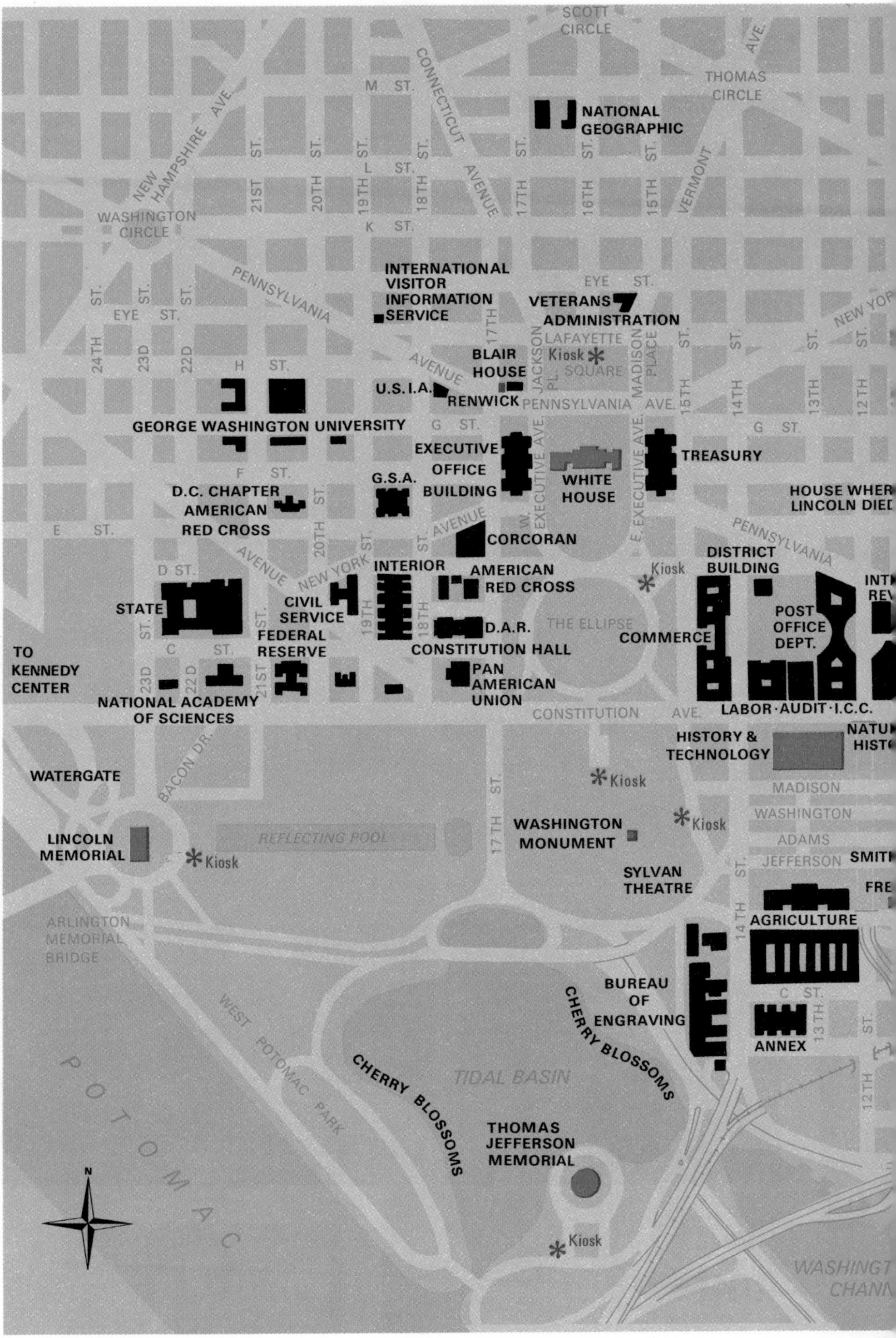

SCOTT CIRCLE
THOMAS CIRCLE
M ST.
L ST.
K ST.
EYE ST.
H ST.
G ST.
F ST.
E ST.
D ST.
C ST.
CONNECTICUT AVENUE
NEW HAMPSHIRE AVE.
VERMONT AVE.
NEW YORK AVE.
PENNSYLVANIA AVENUE
24TH ST.
23D ST.
22D ST.
21ST ST.
20TH ST.
19TH ST.
18TH ST.
17TH ST.
16TH ST.
15TH ST.
14TH ST.
13TH ST.
12TH ST.
WASHINGTON CIRCLE
NATIONAL GEOGRAPHIC
INTERNATIONAL VISITOR INFORMATION SERVICE
VETERANS ADMINISTRATION
LAFAYETTE SQUARE
Kiosk
JACKSON PL.
MADISON PLACE
BLAIR HOUSE
U.S.I.A.
RENWICK
PENNSYLVANIA AVE.
GEORGE WASHINGTON UNIVERSITY
EXECUTIVE OFFICE BUILDING
W. EXECUTIVE AVE.
WHITE HOUSE
E. EXECUTIVE AVE.
TREASURY
HOUSE WHERE LINCOLN DIED
D.C. CHAPTER AMERICAN RED CROSS
G.S.A.
CORCORAN
DISTRICT BUILDING
INTERIOR
AMERICAN RED CROSS
STATE
CIVIL SERVICE
FEDERAL RESERVE
THE ELLIPSE
D.A.R.
CONSTITUTION HALL
COMMERCE
POST OFFICE DEPT.
INTERNAL REVENUE
TO KENNEDY CENTER
NATIONAL ACADEMY OF SCIENCES
PAN AMERICAN UNION
CONSTITUTION AVE.
LABOR · AUDIT · I.C.C.
HISTORY & TECHNOLOGY
NATURAL HISTORY
WATERGATE
BACON DR.
MADISON
WASHINGTON
ADAMS
JEFFERSON
SMITHSONIAN
FREER
LINCOLN MEMORIAL
REFLECTING POOL
WASHINGTON MONUMENT
SYLVAN THEATRE
AGRICULTURE
ARLINGTON MEMORIAL BRIDGE
BUREAU OF ENGRAVING
CHERRY BLOSSOMS
ANNEX
WEST POTOMAC PARK
TIDAL BASIN
THOMAS JEFFERSON MEMORIAL
POTOMAC
N
WASHINGTON CHANNEL

Detach here for poster.

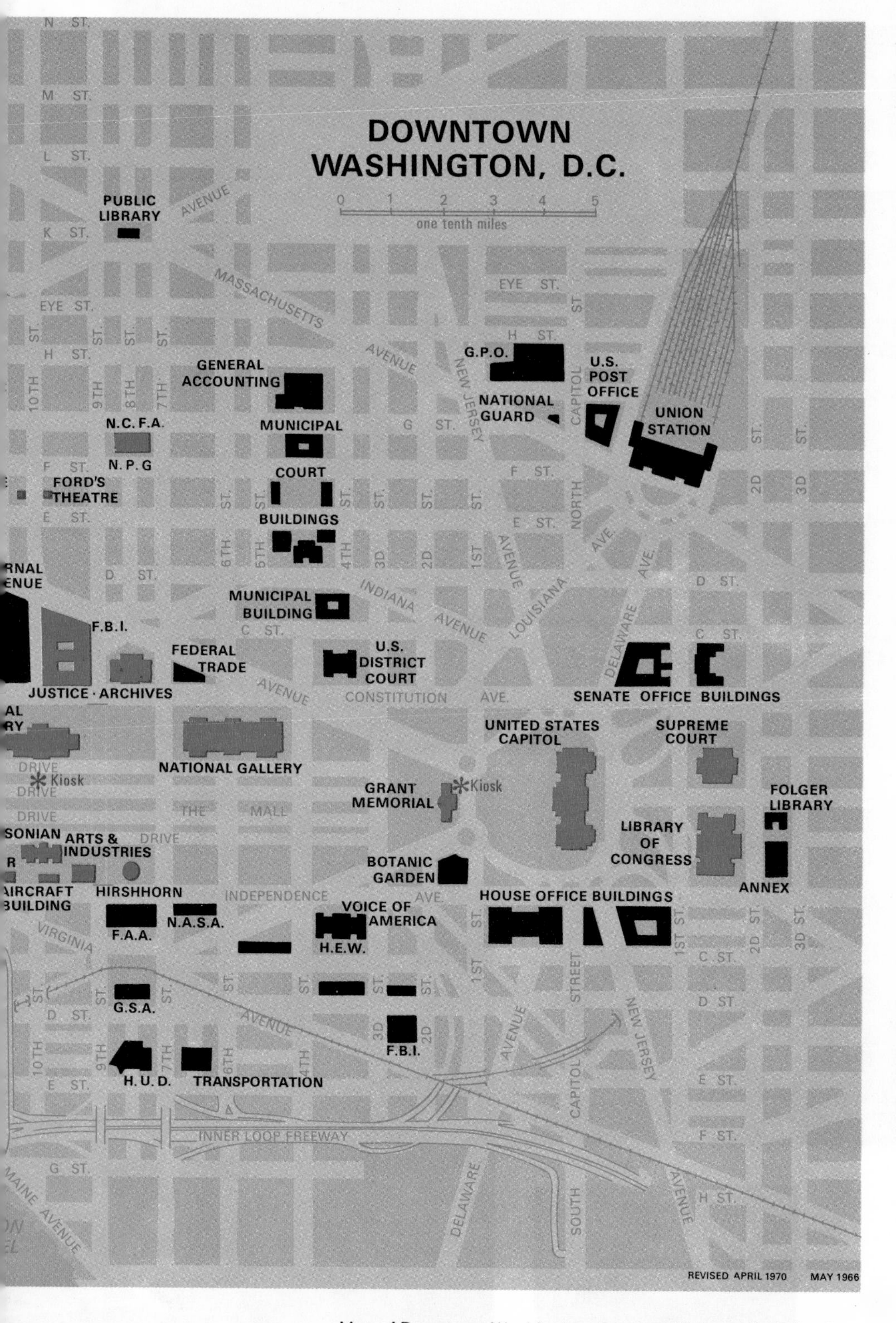

Map of Downtown Washington. Courtesy National Park Service.